With a highly practical and no-nonsense approach (with little use of educational jargon thank goodness). Dr Teys has highlighted the joys of being an independent school principal with his particularly sound advice on the complexities of the role. Theory is illustrated with real examples from his successful career and doctoral research. It is particularly recommended for relatively new principals or aspiring principals.

Dr David Mulford, School Leadership Consultant

As an aspirant principal, I thoroughly enjoyed learning more about the challenges, complexity, opportunity and rewards of contemporary principalship. Dr Teys provides comprehensive insights and shares authentic inner and outer leadership reflections which will support educational leaders to understand and navigate the myriad of complexities of the role of principal more deeply. I strongly recommend this as a must-read for aspirant and early-career principals – in fact, principals in general!

Scott Downward, Head of Teaching and Learning

This book provides excellent guidance to aspiring principals, providing advice and sharing anecdotes about aspects of a principalship which are not often understood by those of us, not in the hot seat. Paul draws on his own experiences, as well as utilising the stories from other principals who were involved in his doctoral thesis, to provide colourful examples which help to illustrate the complex layers associated with leading a school.

Gordon Oldham, Deputy Head of School and Head of Secondary

An honest and heartfelt account, Paul's book provides an easy to read, no nonsense approach for CEOs to shape their own unique leadership style. Paul draws on his own experience to discuss the foundations of leadership, the complex challenges faced by leaders today, and importantly, he articulates the joy and rewards which come from his passionate approach to leadership. A thoroughly compelling and enjoyable read.

Rachel Thomas, CEO Canberra Symphony Orchestra

So you want to be a

PRINCIPAL

So you want to be a

PRINCIPAL

From ideation to success

DR PAUL TEYS

amba
press

Published by Amba Press
Melbourne, Australia
www.ambapress.com.au

Editor – Kathryn Tafra
Cover Designer – Alissa Dinallo

Printed by IngramSpark

ISBN: 9781922607249 (pbk)
ISBN: 9781922607256 (ebk)

A catalogue record for this book is available from the National Library of Australia.

CONTENTS

INTRODUCTION

In 2021 I was awarded a Doctor of Education, conferred following the submission and assessment of my thesis: *Leading large, P-12, autonomous, independent schools: An Australian case study.* The primary purpose of my study was to investigate the leadership, values and perceptions of effectiveness of principals in Australian independent schools. The study examined what is required for principals to be effective, and its findings had far-reaching implications. I could see the potential benefits this knowledge would bring to individual principals, principal preparation programs and professional development and leaning programs. And, most importantly, for the development of the next generation of independent school principals in this country. But how to best share this vital information? Write a book!

I have been a teacher/principal for 38 years, and along the way have gathered experiences, knowledge, understandings, practices and anecdotes. For some time I have been eager to share these with aspiring principals to support their principalship journey. I wanted to assist middle and senior leaders in independent schools to understand how independent schools operate and run. But how best to share my experience and encourage the next generation of school leadership? Write a book!

And so, with the drive of this dual motivation behind me, I have shaped my academic and personal experience into a handbook to guide and inspire principals of the future. When middle leaders have a strong understanding of how things work and how leadership is enacted, they can provide powerful support and assistance to principals, which in turn benefits children and young adults – the reason for our being. This book packages up my experiences and understandings in a way that I hope will support early career principals and experienced principals be more effective in their work.

I hope my story uplifts and inspires anyone who loves their work in schools as much as I do.

Chapter 1

IDEATION

THE LIGHT BULB MOMENT

As a child, I lived with my parents in Wallumbilla, a small country town in western Queensland with not more than 100 people in the whole shire. I attended the local public school. Our principal was a family friend, the late Mr John Ratcliffe.

I remember Mr Ratcliffe moving around our small school; he knew everyone's name, and we felt safe and secure in the knowledge that he was looking after us. He was a commanding presence – you knew when he was nearby, even if you couldn't see him. Nothing was too hard for Mr Ratcliffe; we would ask for things we felt we needed, and he would deliver. He was always keen to chat, make you laugh, and tell you stories that helped you learn, grow and understand the world.

On 20 July 1969, when I was seven years old, American astronauts Neil Armstrong and Edwin "Buzz" Aldrin became the first humans ever to walk on the moon, I watched the Apollo 11 landing on a black and white TV in Mr Ratcliffe's living room. For me, as for so many at the time, the event was inspiring and formative – laying the foundation for my interest in science. That my school principal gave me the unique opportunity to watch the landing in his own home piqued my interest in the role of a school principal.

Although I didn't take deliberate or purposeful steps through my childhood to realise my dream of becoming a principal, my preparation was underway. When I was ten, my father and mother decided we needed to leave Wallumbilla and move closer to the big smoke to get me and my siblings access to a better education. We moved to Allora on the Southern Downs of Queensland, a 40-minute drive to the major city of Toowoomba. Toowoomba was, and is, a renowned education centre with a university and an incredible choice of high-quality public, Catholic and independent schools. Without me consciously knowing it, some sensational teachers there would map my journey to fulfil my dream.

Mr Noel Parsons, my science teacher from years 7–10 at Allora State School, made every lesson theatre. His excitement and passion for his subject were infectious, and his interest in us as human beings was life changing. He offered Swedish massage as a co-curricular activity after school every week. It was well attended and fun, and we learned memorable lessons. Our French teacher and debating coach, Mrs Cathy Cowley, was terrific. She took genuine interest in every one of us, but not just in class – she wanted to know who we were as people and what we did on weekends, to see we were busily involved in our community.

A life-changing event occurred at the end of year 10 and the start of year 11 that confirmed my light bulb moment. Allora State School only went up to year 10, after which students had to change schools, generally to either Warwick High School or Clifton High School. My parents chose Clifton High School because it was a smaller school. They felt I would get lost in the crowd at Warwick High School and not get the personal development they wanted for me.

The guidance officer at the time, who shall remain nameless, sat down with me and decided my subject choices. That was how it was done in 1976 – you were told what your interests were and what you were good at. He told me that I should study English, social mathematics (affectionately known as soggy maths), geometrical drawing, geography, biology, and some other subject I can't remember today. Apologies to the teachers of the subjects mentioned above, but those choices didn't cut it with me. I wanted to study English, maths I and maths II, physics, chemistry and biology – because I wanted to be a maths/science teacher. The guidance officer told me I couldn't study those subjects because my grades in maths and science in year 10 weren't good enough. My mother and I took the subject selection form and headed to enrolment at Clifton High School. Our enrolment interview was with the affable principal Mr George Cominos.

Mr Cominos endeared himself to me from the first handshake. He was immediately interested in me, who I was, my sporting and speaking interests and what I wanted to be when I left his care. I told him I wanted to be a teacher, a maths/science teacher. He said, "Well, why on earth are you choosing these subjects?"

My mother, who was and is to this day my biggest fan, interjected in a tone that was somewhat dismissive of the guidance officer, "Because the guidance officer told him he couldn't be a teacher and said he had to choose these subjects."

Mr Cominos turned to me and said, "Lad, what do you want to do?"

I wanted to be a principal. And as they say, the rest is history.

In hindsight

Mr Cominos was instrumental in permitting me to see my best self in decisions that I might make about my aspirations. He did more than that though, he made sure that my aspirations would be fulfilled through his own personal effort. He was modelling for me what it was to be a great principal and what mattered most in schools for children and young adults.

When the light bulb turns on for you, be ready to see its light and what that light shows you about yourself and your future. Follow your light. It takes courage, and therein lies one of the most important traits of an effective principal.

When setting career goals, take stock of your interests, your values and beliefs, the skills and traits that you have, and how these can help you decide on what is the best career for you. Brainstorm possibilities for you by scanning job sites on a regular basis. Once you have a tentative idea, dive more deeply into these positions and see what is involved. What jobs are worth considering? Read up about the jobs and speak to people who are in the jobs. Consider a day with a person in the role you are considering. Then, make your decision.

CONFIRMATION THAT YOU WANT TO BE A PRINCIPAL

Mr Cominos taught me valuable lessons about leadership and life. He showed me the influence that a principal could have on the life of a young adult. He showed me that I could be who I wanted to be, if I had the desire, commitment and determination to do so. For the two years he was my principal, on every occasion we crossed paths he would stop and speak with me. He would spend time just chewing the fat, hanging out for a few minutes with my mates and me. He was a good communicator, he knew how to use humour to connect with his students. He had a huge smile and his eyes would light up when we were talking about something that appealed to him. If we asked for something we felt the school needed, he would provide it.

At Clifton High, I had incredible teachers who couldn't do enough for us as young adults. Mr Paul Dooley (physics teacher) would drive us to Toowoomba and Warwick so we could play volleyball. Mr Bob Beardsley (science) would take us all over the state – and even to New Zealand – for basketball. Because Allora State School only went to year 10, Ms Vanessa Drew (music teacher) would drive us to and from Allora daily to attend Clifton High. Without me being aware of it, these teachers were shaping me and the principal I would become. As I reflect on my journey, I am now aware that the values and beliefs I formed as a teacher and then a principal were shaped in my own school days. These teachers cared about me as a person. They wanted to give me every opportunity they could; they were most interested in building relationships first, before academic teaching; and they did all they could, outside of usual hours, to give me any practical support and assistance I needed.

I got to study the subjects I wanted and graduated from year 12 at Clifton High School with the equivalent of an ATAR of 95 in today's terms. I went on to study a Bachelor of Applied Science at the University of Southern Queensland (Toowoomba).

For the last two years of my science degree in Toowoomba, I was employed by Toowoomba Grammar School (TGS) as a boarding housemaster, supervising year 9 and 10 boarders in Boyce House. I was given incredible opportunities by staff at TGS who were crucial influences to me: John Winn ensured I coached rugby and cricket; Russell Gillies introduced me to tutoring at the school. I was given an array of opportunities and their leadership inspired me.

Immediately following my science degree, I undertook a Diploma of Education (Dip Ed) at the University of Queensland (Brisbane). In August 1983, I was approaching the end of my Dip Ed when my mother sent me a newspaper clipping advertising a teaching job at Toowoomba's Fairholme College. Principal Allan Faragher was looking for several teachers in critical areas; one position was for a maths/physics teacher. I applied with the assistance and support of my physics lecturer at the university, Dr Jim Butler. Dr Jim was another inspiration – I remember him asking why I wanted to be a principal. I explained that I wanted to do more than teach the group of young adults in my classes. I wanted to lead the teachers and support and operational staff and other members of the school community. I wanted to see that every young adult in the schools where I worked would get the very best education possible. Dr Jim listened carefully then responded, "Why would you want to do anything else?"

I didn't think new graduates got positions at prestigious independent schools like Fairholme College. But I counted my blessings and approached the interview with confidence.

The approach Allan took at the interview appealed to me. He didn't have an interview protocol, a set of questions and a schedule neatly crafted by HR; instead, he entered into a robust conversation with me. He didn't need a script; he knew what he wanted in his next maths/physics teacher and in all new teachers to his school – and he focused on that. He wanted someone who could do much more than just teach a subject; he wanted someone who could make sure children and young adults would learn, and someone who would be heavily committed to the school's holistic programs. At the time I was coaching basketball, volleyball, cross country, athletics, debating and public speaking, all of which worked in my favour.

It seemed Allan was as impressed by me in the interview as I was with him. He offered me the job and in 1984 I began my first teaching position. For five years of my time at Fairholme College, I lived in Telara Cottage and managed the study and activities of the year 12 boarders.

In hindsight

It became apparent to me in my first couple of years at Fairholme that Allan was assembling a team of new graduate teachers who would provide Fairholme students with rich, holistic experiences. The team would go on to form a community of supporters and advocates for the school. I could see how the teachers he had appointed were working hard across so many areas beyond their classroom teaching.

Ultimately, the inspiration that Allan Faragher provided every day gave me the confirmation I needed that I wanted to be a principal. Watching Allan, I could visualise myself in the role and imagine how I would enact it. I was forming my values, beliefs and priorities. That moulding and shaping was the most profound activity happening for me at the time.

How can a deputy or aspirant tune in and soak up everything that is happening? Attend as many school events and functions as practically possible – get to understand the school's culture. Coach sporting teams and debating teams, or conduct music ensembles – get to know the students and what they value and appreciate in their school. Put your hand up to lead school committees and advisory groups. Be active in your professional associations by taking on leadership roles in your networks.

THE PREPARATION FOR PRINCIPALSHIP BEGINS

The preparation for becoming a principal begins long before you see the advertisement on LinkedIn, or the head-hunter taps you on the shoulder. Preparation begins early in your career once the idea grabs you.

My preparation began with my first principal, Allan Faragher. I am guessing that, during my early years at Fairholme, Allan saw something in me that made him want to shape my journey without explicitly saying so.

I started as a maths/physics teacher in 1984. Within a couple of years, Allan had asked me to take on the role of head of science, which I accepted with excitement. Not long after that, Allan called me to his office and said he had created a new role, and that I was ideal for the position – head of curriculum. This was an executive leadership position sitting beside the deputy principal and head of students. I would be in charge of everything from curriculum to teacher professional development – it was a significant role, and I was thrilled to accept. I thrived and the school flourished.

It is rare these days to be going into a principal role without a postgraduate qualification. During my time at Fairholme College I realised I would benefit greatly from postgraduate studies. I chose to do a Master of Education with Deakin University, specialising in mathematics education. It served me well, strengthening my knowledge about curriculum and pedagogy in mathematics, which, I felt at the time, I could easily transfer to other subject areas.

The principalship is a highly complex job, and you do need specialist skills to be effective in the role. This is discussed in more detail in chapter 5, "You are the CEO." I now believe that a master in leadership and/or management would be more appropriate for the leadership context in schools in the 2020s. I also recommend doing a Master of Business Administration (MBA). Harvard's graduate Certificate in School Leadership and Management is another good option. Many universities now offer high quality, appropriate and career-serving programs to the aspirant leader, from master degrees to graduate certificates, to help prepare teachers who want to pursue a career as a principal. Tertiary educational leadership courses are designed for aspiring principals, deputy principals and assistant principals, and differ in emphasis depending on the university.

I believe that a postgraduate qualification is an essential passport to principalship in an age where school leaders face intense pressures. It is also a demonstrable sign that you, as a leader of learning, are active, committed and engaged in lifelong learning. It is essential to select the right course. Choose a course that will develop your expertise in education leadership and management and provide you with rich and valuable professional learning that challenges your thinking about leadership.

But let's return to my time at Fairholme. After being at the school for almost fifteen years as principal, Allan decided it was time to retire. I wanted to keep working with him, kicking goals as we had been. I was saddened by his decision – but I was also happy for him. With Allan's retirement I reflected on my own career journey. I had been at Fairholme since I finished my Dip Ed ten years earlier, and I knew that it was time for me to move onwards and upwards.

In the second half of 1994, I applied for the head of secondary role at AB Paterson College, where Dawn Lang was the principal. Like Allan, I guess Dawn saw promise in me – she gave me untold opportunities to lead. My co-head (of primary) was Bill Cunnington and together we were the school's executive leaders.

As a motivated executive, I put a high value on the quality of self-leadership; in order to prepare for the next step in my career I had to focus on self-improvement and professional growth. My leadership journey involved an intentional mix of formal learning, job experience, colleagues and affiliations, and professional reading (any reading that relates to education and educational leadership and has a quality foundation that usually derives from research or extended experience of practitioners). Some elements of my preparation included making commitments to collegial organisations, such as the appropriate Association of Heads of Independent Schools of Australia (AHISA) networks (Deputy Net, for example) and the state-based Associations of Independent Schools. I also made commitments to associations that added value to the student programs, including sporting associations and network groups. For example, when I was principal at Hunter Valley Grammar, I held the position of treasurer at the Hunter Region Independent Schools association. This position was honorary and voluntary, and I held it for twelve years.

Professional development opportunities will give you many of the skills and knowledge needed to perform at a high level. You will also learn much through mentorship and coaching, or just by situational observation. However, contemporary would-be principals ought to have a post-graduate qualification. This will carry weight on an application and have an impact at first glance.

Aside from career benefits and pathways, one of the more overlooked reasons for taking on a postgraduate qualification is to learn more about a particular area of interest. If you are passionate about a particular subject, why not devote yourself to researching and learning more about it? You could even find yourself becoming a subject matter expert.

Post-graduate study is an investment in your personal development and the benefits are not to be underestimated. Further study will help you develop skills that will support your daily work as a principal. These skills include time management, formal research, analytical thinking, historical perspectives, writing and presenting to diverse audiences.

The role of principal is a complex and demanding one, and to manage its requirements and expectations, you need a rigorous learning and development program; this is not something you can skimp on. A voracious appetite for reading is required, as is a commitment to read regularly from within and outside of the fields of education.

How can you learn to be a principal?

An effective principal works with or seeks counsel and advice from a mentor, coach or trusted colleague. They participate in professional leadership networks, collegial and professional associations, and peak bodies. They regularly reflect on their performance, practices, areas of strength and areas to be developed. They use performance appraisals, reviews and feedback, and reflection survey instruments to determine their professional learning needs. They engage in relevant short courses and professional development programs, such as the Australian Institute of Company Directors (AICD) course and courses offered by the CEO Institute.

They attend conferences, professional learning seminars and workshops. They constantly monitor their performance and reflect on their decisions, actions and impact. In essence, they seek professional learning opportunities relevant to their principal preparation context. They are judicious in choosing experiences that will impact their leadership preparation and ensure they are effective in the roles they have along the journey.

During my first principalship, I applied to do a doctorate. However, I wasn't able to make the commitment at that time. I was in my early forties, I had three children aged between five and ten, and my first principalship – an exciting and motivating period in my life – came with a heavy workload. I just couldn't manage the time commitment required. Instead, I dedicated myself to reading widely, networking to learn from colleagues and learning as much as I could about the role by reflecting on daily practice.

In 2014, during my second principalship, I decided to pursue a Doctor of Education.

Reading and networking widely and gaining broad life experiences are key to your preparation to be principal. Of all of the wonderful, rich experiences and relationships I have had, Robin Sharma's book *The 5 AM Club* was the most life changing. Sharma's book *The Monk Who Sold His Ferrari* was equally impactful. The *5 AM Club* delivers on its promise to transform the four pillars of creativity, productivity, prosperity, and service to the world. These four pillars are the cornerstones to a successful principalship.

The *5 AM Club* inspired me and encouraged me to formalise the daily practices that I had been using for many years. The habits I knew worked for me were acknowledged and affirmed by Sharma, and I was able to refine and hone my morning routine based on his teachings. I found I was better organised, achieved more in my day, had higher energy levels and was able to feel a whole lot more content with my work-life balance. It provided me with a reset at an important time in my professional journey, affirming the daily routines I needed to sustain me in my professional life. I have no affiliation with the book's author, but he re-energised me.

You don't have to use Sharma's techniques, but find who/what works for you to ensure you are at your magnificent best – as you will need to be for this role.

I found it very important to develop financial acumen. By poring over monthly financial statements, I began to understand the financial sustainability of the school. I learned to understand the balance sheet and the statement of cash flow. I would not permit myself to sit in finance meetings pretending that I understood the numbers. I wasn't afraid to ask questions of the accountant, the finance director or the auditor to understand what was needed. I would encourage aspiring and early-career principals to do courses on finance through, for example, the Australian Institute of Company Directors (AICD) or the Australian Institute of Management (AIM). I joined both AICD and AIM as a member after I finished at Hunter Valley Grammar School (HVGS) in 2020 to support my professional learning and development as I began my journey as an executive consultant. I only wish I had joined them earlier in my career, as the experience would have only improved the effectiveness of my governance.

What shapes a principal?

When you are ready to start applying for principal roles, it is important to remember that the knowledge, experiences and ideologies you take with you – especially to your first interview – are shaped by your early career learning activities. These might include:

- Pre-service teacher training
- The university you choose for your undergraduate and post-graduate degree
- The reading that you do
- The advice that colleagues and those in the principal role have provided
- The professional networks you establish
- Your choice of mentor
- Conference and meeting activities that you choose.

As a principal, your values and beliefs will be deeply anchored in the training and development you engage in and will be reinforced by the scholarly community you spend time with.

Most important of all when dealing with finances, interrogate the reports. It can be hard as an executive leader to gain access to financial reports. Make it known to your principal that you would like to sit on the finance committee or ask your principal to share a set of reports with you (in confidence).

I was head of secondary at AB Paterson College for four years, during which time I learned an incredible amount from Dawn. In my fourth year, the position of principal at Moreton Bay College became available, and my colleague and good friend Jeff Buchanan encouraged me to apply. Jeff gave me incredible support, helping me craft an application that reflected the qualities and attributes I would bring to the role and showcased the experiences and achievements that demonstrated I was ready for the role. Six months after the application was submitted – at the tender age of thirty-seven – I became the principal of a P–12 girls school with 1200 students.

In hindsight

When you have made the decision that you want to apply for principal positions, it is time to start reviewing principal recruitment prospectuses as part of your preparation. These prospectuses will give you clear insights and understandings about what the role entails and what boards expect of their principal.

If you aren't on seek.com at this stage, register and sign up. Enter "principal" in the keywords search and sit back and wait for the advertised positions to hit your inbox. At this stage, you aren't necessarily applying but reviewing the role description and considering what is required, the skills and competencies you are meant to have, and the necessary acumen that is needed. Many recruiters these days do not put the recruitment prospectus on the web – ask them for one. Study what is required and audit your skills, experience, and competencies to assess whether you are ready to apply.

It is a good time right now in your journey to elicit the services of a mentor to travel with you.

A PURPOSEFUL APPLICATION

When it comes to crafting an application, your current principal can be your best ally and serve as a wealth of knowledge and practical assistance. You might feel reluctant to ask your current principal for help, feeling you might be betraying them, or that they won't support you, or your leaving might cause them distress. However, if you have a solid and trusting relationship with your principal, they will help you and their practical support can serve you well.

If your principal is reluctant or doesn't have the requisite skills or interest, it may be worth engaging your own professional mentor. A coach or mentor can do wonders for you on the purposeful journey to applying. There are two approaches I would recommend when finding a professional mentor: using an active LinkedIn profile to engage with mentors in educational leadership, and reaching out to the professional associations of educational leaders and asking them who works in the field.

You can expect a mentor to provide unbiased feedback on your application and resume; to suggest courses or programs to attend to fill gaps in your experience; to help keep your morale up when you are discouraged. They can bring a fresh, independent perspective to your work; enhance and further your current qualities and skills; help you identify goals, prioritise them and choose the right path to achieve them; and provide a confidential and supportive sounding board.

Recruitment specialists can also assist you. They will have their name and contact details attached to advertising for principal and executive positions, so should be easy to find. All principal positions in Australia are being managed by recruitment specialists. Make yourself known to them and tell them that you are interested in a principalship, and they can assist.

Don't consider submitting an application until you are ready and have found a school that is the right fit. You will know you are ready for the step to being a principal when your interest in the role grows, your belief in your capacity to do the job becomes stronger, you find yourself talking to your principal about the role, you attend conferences and are inspired by those doing the job, and your colleagues begin talking to you about your suitability and readiness. If you have an active LinkedIn profile, the recruiters will reach out to you when they think you are ready.

An application usually requires: a cover letter, resume and response to the key selection criteria.

The application

For all principal positions, an information package is developed to provide all of the information that you should want, including clear guidelines on how to apply. Be sure to follow the requirements conscientiously. And be sure to let the recruiter – hired to manage the appointment on behalf of the board – know who you are as a leader, a person, and the school's next principal.

The cover letter

The cover letter you include with your resume is often as important as the resume itself. In your cover letter, include an eye-catching and powerful introduction followed by your relevant experience and executive expertise. Include achievements and skills in your cover letter and finish it with a positive and persuasive statement.

Keep it to one page or less and don't load it up by using narrow margins or small font. Use normal A4 margins and a contemporary 11-point font.

When applying to be a principal you will be competing with others who will also have impressive work histories and plentiful accomplishments. Your cover letter needs to intrigue the recruiter so that they will spend more time reading your resume and learning about why you are the right person for the principal position.

Don't use the cover letter templates you find on the web. They are a dime a dozen – and they are not you. The recruiter can tell when someone has used a template cover letter or resume, and it won't make a favourable impression.

The resume

The application instructions may limit the number of pages your resume should be. If not, keep your resume to two or three pages.

I worked to ensure that my resume portrayed leadership, authority and professionalism. I knew that I had to create the strong and professional resume of a principal to make sure my application passed through a recruiter's processes and into the hands of the "real" employer, the board chair and board.

When applying for a principal position, remember that the other contenders will have put as much work into it as you. You have to be better!

Your resume must successfully present *you* and *your capabilities*. Your resume needs to tell a narrative about you.

From my experience – and my successful applications – here are my tips for an exemplary resume:

Include a profile statement

A profile statement is a great way to quickly give the recruiter or board of directors an introduction to you and your executive skills. This statement should only be a few sentences long and should include your experience as an executive leader, your management skills as they relate to the position you are applying for and examples of leadership in your background. You can also include any achievements that relate to the position you are applying for.

Highlight achievements that are related to management

Achievements trump lists. While you may have a number of impressive achievements, it's important to only include those that are relevant to the school and position you are applying for and that portray your management abilities. When writing about your achievements, be sure to use numbers so that hiring managers have a concrete idea of the impact you made.

Use keywords when listing your skills

It is important to demonstrate that you have the skills and abilities listed in the information package. This increases your chances of making it past the application screening system and getting noticed by a potential employer. Include keywords from the information package when listing your skills. I also like to use phrases like, "My colleagues have described me as…" Or, "I have become known by my colleagues as…" Or, "My referees would attest to…" This gives the feeling of an outsider perspective to my skills.

Consider including extra sections

While education, experience and skills are the most important components of a principal's resume, you may want to include additional sections to further highlight your capabilities and skills as they relate to a principal position. Keep in mind that any extra sections you include should be directly related to the position you are applying for.

Your resume should be carefully structured to quickly convey information to those reading it.

Format your resume

Keeping your resume as clear and easy-to-read as possible is important to ensure that employers can quickly see what makes you a good candidate for a position. Begin with your contact details, use appropriate heading font size and chronologically format your resume for easy reading.

Professional summary or profile

As mentioned earlier, a summary or objective can help to grab the attention of hiring companies. Use a resume summary if you have more than two years of experience as a CEO or related position and use a resume objective if you have less experience.

Education and academic qualifications

Start with the highest qualification and move through each formal academic qualification in turn. The order of each entry should go: Qualification, University, Year graduated, Single sentence illustrating the core course outcome.

Recent and relevant professional development

Include relevant coursework that you have completed beyond formal academic qualifications. This can help make your education section stand out from other candidates.

Employment history

Begin with your current or most recent position. The order of each entry should go: Role title, school name, dates of employment, five to seven bullet points of your responsibilities.

Achievements

This section has become more important in recent years as boards want to know about your achievements that added value to your current school's programs and services.

Skills and traits

Determine the most appropriate skills and traits to include. As mentioned earlier, including relevant and appropriate skills related to the principal position you are applying for can boost your chances of having your resume seen by hiring managers.

Referees

While it is commonplace now to make a statement to the effect of "Referees are available upon request", it is more effective to list your referees, with your current principal at the top of the list.

Response to the key selection criteria

It has become common for the information package that forms a crucial part of the recruitment to contain general and specific criteria that an applicant must address.

I have extracted from a recent principal appointment information package (March 2022) the key selection criteria used. While each school will have nuanced differences, they will usually look something like this:

> The Principal is the Chief Executive Officer and is responsible to the Board for the strategic direction and operational leadership of [school].
>
> Candidates must be able to demonstrate the following attributes:
>
> - A passion for excellence and innovation in education and for continuous learning
> - The ability to inspire enthusiasm, pride and loyalty throughout the school community
> - The ability to provide outstanding academic, strategic and operational leadership and a high level of staff engagement
> - A knowledge and understanding of emerging trends in education and education management practice
> - Exceptional communication and relationship building skills
> - Outstanding personal qualities of openness, integrity, energy, and leadership coupled with self-confidence and a balanced perspective.

Ensure you address each point clearly and succinctly, tying it to the narrative that will distinguish you from other applicants.

Interview preparation

If your application is successful, you will progress to the interview rounds (more on this in the following sections). Before you reach this point, I would recommend developing a personal leadership mission statement. Much like a corporate mission statement, this will describe your convictions, what you stand for, and how you plan to create a life that embodies your values. In other words, it will become your personal definition of success.

You will be far more successful in an interview if you know who you are as a leader, what your values and beliefs are, and what you will hold steadfast to in the role.

Your personal mission statement should be short, usually a sentence or two, and point to the direction you intend your leadership to take you. It's like a compass that helps you stay on track, heading in the direction you want to go.

Finding your personal leadership mission statement

It can be difficult to articulate your mission statement without feedback or coaching, or the ability to self-reflect. This exercise will guide you.

Brainstorm your "why", thinking about the following:

- What inspires you and gets you out of bed in the morning?
- What are your innate strengths?
- How will you measure success in your life?
- What do you stand for? What do you stand against?
- What setbacks have you experienced and what have they taught you?
- What values or positive character traits or skills do you want to develop further?
- What phrases guide your everyday actions?
- What important relationships do you want to cultivate in your life?
- How do you want to feel each day?

Look over the results of your brainstorm; note common threads and themes. Write no more than a paragraph summarising your brainstorm results.

If necessary, condense your paragraph. Condense it again as many times as needed. Keep refining your personal leadership mission statement until it is clear and brief – no more than three sentences long.

It may help to leave some time between each of the steps outlined here – this process should not be rushed. Similarly, it may help to think about aspects of the exercise in different places (while walking, or in the bath). You may be surprised by what comes up when you are in a different place or mode to usual.

Defining your "why" and becoming crystal clear on the larger purpose fuelling your leadership self will help you prepare for an interview and, when in the role, will be the anchor that helps you ride out changes and future setbacks.

When the interview panel start asking you some of those tougher questions about your philosophy, drawing on your personal leadership mission statement will help you believe in yourself and respond to the questions with confidence.

When developing your leadership identity think about what your colleagues, followers and the community can consistently expect from you. How will they know you, what will you stand for, what can they rely on you for, how will you build trust and confidence? How visible will your leadership be? One thing all influential leaders have in common is a clear, visible leadership identity that they are true to. Your identity must show up for the interview panel, it could be the favourable difference between you and other equally suitable candidates.

Know what you are good at, understand your leadership context, know when you thrive (and wither), know your abilities (and shortcomings), know how you want to be perceived. Shape your identity from these reflections.

The risk if you don't have or know your leadership identity is that you will fall to others' views of you and how they perceive you. Take charge of what sort of leader you want to be – don't let others define you. Have a strong inner voice as your compass.

THE RIGHT FIT

I have seen principals' careers perish because they chose the wrong school. In the excitement of applying for your first or subsequent principalship, or after you have been passed over for job offers, it can be easy to forget to evaluate the fit. This can create a perilous tenure. It is so hard for a new principal if the school is not the right fit. While boards do their due diligence to find a suitable principal, an applicant principal must assess whether the school they are considering is the right fit for them.

To do this, visit the school, pore over its website, make note of the key messages that describe the school's values and beliefs, ask colleagues or the national and state associations what they know about the school. Form your own view about the school's ethos, general profile and reputation, and gather as much knowledge as possible. Make a considered decision at this point – do you want to apply?

Eighty per cent of independent schools are faith based, and principals have to make commitments to the relevant affiliate church bodies. Each one of the case study principals in my doctoral research spoke of the value of these organisations and the commitments they made to them. You have to do this in a church school or Christian school – it would be hypocritical to accept a position in these schools and not commit to church life outside of school hours. Moreover, it would be hard to lead effectively if you were not a person of committed faith.

I have to say that in my experience the church schools caused some of my colleagues the greatest grief. The bishop, a rule unto himself, would rule with a unilateral fist, without regard for democratic practices. The layers of governance that exists in church schools makes governance by the local board problematic.

There is also an inherent problem in the recruitment process if the board do not do their homework. I have seen principals and executive leaders appointed without the recruiting board contacting the board chair or the principal of the applicant's current school. This is very poor form and can result in an unsuccessful appointment.

I have seen principals so keen to get their first principalship that they are less than honest about who they are, their values, beliefs and philosophies, just to get the job. My colleague David calls this "white line fever", aka stepping over the "white line". An individual acts out in ways that are not true to themselves. They will say anything to get the job. Be sure, as an aspirant, that you choose a school where you are good fit.

The modus operandi in the 2020s is for the recruiter (more aptly the head-hunter) to purposefully and strategically choose a principal to match the needs and aspirations of the school at that point in the school's history.

Significant family support

Significant family support is essential to the application process and the principalship. You can't contemplate applying unless your partner is willing to support you practically and psychologically. The job is demanding of you and your family.

Your partner can be your moral strength. It can be lonely at the top if you don't have someone with whom you can share your struggles, doubts and worries. Your partner can help you commit to the role as they show interest in your work and school. You become a team. As principal, you will need a trusted ear to unload your thoughts and concerns. Your partner can be the voice of perspective. This levelling influence is invaluable to a principal, and what better source for it than the person you can trust the most.

It is vital to communicate with your partner about how your work is affecting the family. Most principals I know have good intentions with the time and energy they pour into work; they feel they are doing it for their families. My experience is that principals still spend more time in the school and on school-related business than with their partner and children, which is taxing on the family. Be mindful of this so your partner doesn't become jealous of the school or resentful of your time in the school. You have to be in it together.

The recruiter

The recruitment specialist is engaged by the board of a school seeking a new principal to manage all aspects of the recruitment process. Recruiters are active on LinkedIn and across the digital landscape, searching for and growing their database of potential applicants.

Recruiters help school boards find the right person for a particular role. They work to assemble a pool of applicants for the board to review by researching potential contacts, interviewing candidates, and building a network of top-tier talent within their candidate pool.

Recruiters use hiring software and networking databases to seek talent nationally and internationally. They keep a sharp eye on key players in the education industry and are always aware of top talent, and any vacancies in the market.

Recruiters have a strong knowledge of the requirements for any principal position and are the effective mouthpiece for what the school wants in their next principal. They will typically conduct a screening interview and ask important baseline questions that assess your fit for the role. They then make recommendations to the board for further interviews.

Recruiters manage all job listings and monitor incoming applications. They are the first point of contact between a school and you. They are instrumental in your chances of success.

In hindsight

When you find a role that is a good fit, seek the help of a mentor to support you through the application process. Ask your mentor to review your resume and cover letter, and to coach you through any interviews you might be invited to attend. Get some support for the application part of the process and, if successful, for the interview. Your mentor can provide sample questions and conduct practise interviews with you.

I can't stress how important it is that you elicit the support of experienced and trusted colleagues to assist you with the application process. The recruiters are the gatekeepers – they read hundreds of applications. They know what a stock application looks like; they will set yours aside if it is common. They know what needs to be included as a minimum to be competent. Follow the advice in this section and you will meet their requirements. In your application, having covered all of the mandated requirements, make sure you tell your story: who you are, where you've come from, and what you stand for.

Remember, if it is meant to be – it will be.

THE INTERVIEW, OFFER AND CONTRACT

You've had a call from the recruiter, and you have been offered an interview. It is highly probable that the first interview will be conducted by the recruiter and a member of their team. It probably will not involve anyone from the school or school board.

The first interview for a job is the most critical because it determines if you get past the gatekeeper, a recruiter who, I might add, has probably never, ever been a principal. Capitalising on ways to leave a unique impression on the recruiter will accelerate you through the interview process and propel you into the ranks of candidate-of-choice. Leading with an intentional, confident interview strategy can change the trajectory of your job search, making you the strongest candidate by differentiating you from your competition.

Prepare as assiduously as you can for this first interview. Don't assume you will progress any further. Hiring decisions are made during the interview process, yet many applicants take a passive approach, failing to adequately prepare a strategy to distinguish themselves from the other applicants, leaving much of the outcome up to chance. Needless to say, this is unwise.

First interview tips

Prior to the interview, do in-depth research into the school. Go beyond its website content to uncover its core values and strengths, and speak to these in the interview.

During the interview, ask insightful questions that display your understanding of the position's requirements. Take a deeper dive into what the greatest challenges of the role will be and ask about the milestones that will measure your success.

Prepare specific examples that demonstrate how your core strengths align with the skills, experience and purpose of the position. This is often where interviewees get tripped up and lack confidence to speak about themselves, so capitalise on this opportunity and tell the stories that allow you to shine. Remember, it's not bragging if it's true.

Call out the elephant in the room. Whether it is your lack of experience, qualifications or apparent expertise, don't wait for the interviewer to mention it. Instead, prepare a statement describing how you intend to bridge any gaps that exist and effectively move forward. Being the first to raise the topic demonstrates your professional transparency and confidence to anticipate and address what they may be concerned about.

Be yourself! Above all else, be true to yourself, let your light shine.

Remember to send a thank-you note after the interview, reflecting on the conversation. Customise your message to address any issues that remain outstanding, or that you felt were not communicated clearly on your end. This may be your last opportunity to influence the interviewer's decision. Don't be shy; if you really want the job, ask for it.

When the first interview is behind you, you will hopefully be called and offered a second interview. This could well be with the whole board; if not the full board, there could be a panel of five or more. My advice in preparing for this second interview is to relax, don't over-prepare. Trust your instincts, insights and experience to buttress you for a good interview. Be yourself and try and connect at a deeper level with individual panel members. Show your character, let the panel know the real you. Establishing rapport is your aim.

If you find yourself invited to a final interview, down to the last two, prepare yourself for the unexpected.

I recall being invited to a second and final interview where, as part of a series of trials on the day, I was required to present to a packed lecture theatre attended by all board members, representatives of the past students association, and current staff. This was pretty intense, so I went to the school the day before and met with the deputy and head of IT – it was in the late nineties and I wanted to test the technology in the theatre. Everything worked seamlessly and I enjoyed chatting to the two senior staff. I asked the deputy if he had any advice for me. The deputy was older than me and advised me, *be yourself!*

After being appointed to the role, I learned that the other finalist did not visit the school before her presentation, and guess what? The technology failed her. She had to present without technology. It was costly for her.

Unbeknown to me at the time, at that presentation sat a board member who had also applied for the principal position. He did not get an interview. I didn't know who he was, but noticed he threw a few ridiculous questions at me. I smelt a rat but couldn't be sure. In one question he referred to a seminal work about the future of Australian schools, claiming any educator worth their salt would know of it. He used the fictitious article to try and discredit a point I was making. I knew he was full of nonsense so I called him out on it, offering another piece of research – which I knew the educators in the room would certainly know about – to try and trump him. The board chair told me at dinner that I was successful.

As part of the selection process, you and your partner could be required to attend a dinner or luncheon with the board. I recall at one such dinner the meals were served and we were all set to eat. There was a pregnant pause, an eerie pause. I was clueless as to why...

After I was appointed, the board chair told me that the "pause" was deliberate. It was to give me time to say grace. I failed that test – but I still got the job.

The board chair had asked me an odd question at dinner: "How did you find your accommodation?"

I thought it odd because I was staying in one of the city's finest five-star hotels. Given the school had booked and paid for it, there was only one answer – "Excellent, really good, and thank you for arranging it."

The chair went on, "That's good to hear, the other applicant asked to be moved!"

I think back and wonder if that other applicant "lost" the position, rather than me "winning" it.

Finally, if you are going really well, you will get the call from the board chair or the recruiter, verbally offering you the position.

Get excited but contain your excitement. And wait until you have a contract in hand before you start sharing your successful appointment too widely. There may be some verbal negotiating about terms and conditions; it would be wise to play your cards close to your chest and not agree to anything until you have a contract in writing.

Speak to your current head about the appropriate salary. AHISA do a twice-yearly salary survey to get benchmarking data for principals in independent schools. Your current principal can help with the contract inclusions and clauses.

When you have a written contract, engage an employment lawyer who works in the independent schools' sector. AHISA, is an excellent resource at this time, reach out to them. It is important to get the contract right at the time of negotiation; it is so hard to change a contract once you have been appointed. There are traps for young players, so get advice from an employment lawyer. Contact the CEO of AHISA and ask if they can put you in touch with someone suitable.

It is ok to take several days or a week before you accept. Take your time, but don't labour accepting the offer – this can create the perception that you can't make decisions, and you don't want that.

Read the contract carefully yourself, before you get legal advice. You need to know how to read contracts and legal documents; it is a part of your work. Pay attention to each clause.

As part of the negotiation, arrange a start date that works for you. You want to get a break between your current role and your new role. Try and achieve a four-week break. You will need it. You want to start the principal role refreshed, rested and with a keen, sharp mind.

In hindsight

This is a stressful period, try to let the process run its course naturally. Build a positive relationship with the recruiter, stay close to them without becoming annoying. You might find yourself involved in several misfires, unsuccessful applications. You might not get your first one and may have to apply again, and again. This is part of the process. Don't let it deter you, it is normal. Don't be hard on yourself if you are unsuccessful, dust yourself off, regroup, reflect on the lessons to be learned. Do ask for feedback. What is important is that you treat your next application as a new one. Don't simply resurrect your prior application. Use it as a base, but refresh it substantially for the context of the next position.

PRIOR TO TAKING UP THE NEW ROLE

Announce your departure to your current boss (and colleagues)

You've nailed the interview, negotiated your salary, and just signed on the dotted line to accept your new job. Now, there's just one minor issue standing in the way of your highly anticipated new gig: your old one.

It is important for immediate family members to hear your good news first. Once you've shared the exciting news with them, be sure to tell your current boss you'll be leaving before you tell colleagues or anyone else. You may be eager to let everyone know about the new opportunities or changes in your life but be sure you tell your boss first. The last thing you want is for your boss to hear that you're leaving through one of your colleagues or through one of his/her colleagues. As soon as you have made the decision to accept your offer, set up a meeting with your boss to discuss your new appointment and the work to be done before you go. This is a show of respect and professionalism. While it may seem obvious, plenty have stuffed this up, making their departure more stressful.

Having a plan for finalising your relationships with your boss and colleagues can solidify their favourable perceptions about you and help you get good references for the future. It is important that you don't damage relationships, which can reappear many years later in different forms. If you plan your exit well, you'll be able to leave on good terms and in the school's good graces. That's always the best way to move on from a job, especially since you may even end up working with some of your former colleagues or previous boss at other jobs in the future. It is uncanny how many people from my past have popped up in unexpected places – I have appointed teachers of mine to positions in schools where I was a principal/executive leader. I have had colleagues turn up on boards. I even had a former close colleague appear on the selection panel for my second principalship. I am so glad I didn't burn any bridges – it would have made things so much harder for myself. Of course, this isn't just advice for when you leave a position, it applies to working relationships in general.

Thank those who had a positive impact on you

Resist the temptation to celebrate your good fortune of landing a new job too enthusiastically at work. You will only alienate your soon-to-be former boss and colleagues. Be gracious, take the time to thank everyone who has helped you to be productive in your role. Your generosity and modesty will be remembered. Single people out and express your gratitude for their support at any going-away parties. Take the time to send a goodbye email to the people you've worked with, including colleagues, clients, parents, and people working in the business partnerships you have forged.

Your current colleagues will be happy for you and will congratulate you, but they will also harbour feelings of sadness and regret – they will miss you. Accept the invitations from friends and colleagues to have small parties or farewells. It is an important part of the separation and, if done well, will ensure that any anxiety can be minimised.

Relationships you have formed in your current role can be sustaining, long lasting and beneficial to you in the future. If there's anyone at your current work or associated with your current role who you'd like to continue to stay in touch with, get their contact information before leaving.

Write a transition plan

Putting together a transition plan is a great way to stay organised and ensure you have enough time to complete your remaining tasks before leaving your current job. It also leaves a great impression with your employer. Write down all of the specific tasks you will do before leaving your position, including administrative tasks, and the amount of time it will take you to do them. Then, make a list of who will own your projects and tasks once you leave, and write down the dates that these handovers will take place.

Your employer will appreciate the effort and let you know if there are any issues with this timeline. The extra planning will also help you set realistic goals for your last few weeks.

Make a personal budget for your transition to the new role – you may be moving to a new town or a new suburb, consider the costs around a new home, relocation, etc. Your next school might be generous with your salary and conditions, or they might be mean-spirited (hopefully not). You will have negotiated your contract so you will know what your new salary will be. Create a household budget to fit your new salary. But be prudent about this in the early stages of enjoying your salary. You will be earning a different income than usual, creating a plan for your budget helps take away some of the uncertainty.

Matters to attend to (well) before you finish

It is perfectly reasonable, and being responsible to yourself, to take copies of your important work and documents. There is no need to do this in a secretive way but do it discretely. Do take your intellectual property with you, along with anything you feel will be useful in the future. Take all those important contacts and connections you know you will need in the future, including contact information for the colleagues you want to stay in touch with.

I have seen colleagues escorted from their office and asked to box up personal items, I have witnessed boards cutting off computer access when a staff member announced they were leaving. Be mindful of this. It is an awful thought to harbour but be aware it can happen, and be prepared. No matter what you've been doing on your work phone and computer, wipe them of any personal or non-work-related information before giving them back. This not only helps protect your privacy, but it makes the job of redistributing these devices much easier. Delete any software you downloaded on these devices that wasn't strictly meant for this job. Save any files or emails externally, then clear them from the device. Delete your browsing history, cookies, and any saved autofill information. This is important to do – there is nothing clandestine in this, it's just good ICT practice.

Go out of your way to leave on good terms. I know at least one person will need to hear this: your final two weeks is not the time to go around your workplace telling everyone what you really think of them. There's bound to be at least one person you clashed with during your time at this job, but now's the time to take the high road. Do not badmouth management or staff. People have long memories when it comes to criticism, and you never know when inquiries about your performance will be made by future employers. Even if you hated your job or your boss, there's no point in saying so.

Give as much notice as possible, I don't mean official notice, but notice of when your last day in the office will be. Give at least four weeks and stick to it but, ideally, give as much notice as you can.

For the sake of those who are happy for you and encouraged you to apply for your new job, try and keep things light and positive in your last days at work. If you landed a great new position, be humble about it. Move on to better things quietly and politely.

Once everything is officially over with, make sure you plan some time for a celebration or just some good, relaxing time off. This could be a week off for a lavish vacation or a nice dinner. Anything that helps you commemorate the time spent and allows you space to prepare to move on to new opportunities. Plan something fun for yourself after your last day and celebrate all the things you have learned since you first started.

The transition to your new position

Before taking up your new position, do keep in touch with the principal or board chair at your new school. Keep across any developments or plans that are being rolled out, especially if you will need to adopt or implement them. Do speak up if you have any concerns. Don't stay silent if something does not sit well with you. Subliminally you are declaring how you will do things when you are the boss - so show your courage and speak up.

There are three important areas at your new school where I recommend you get involved:

1. Staff appointments that will impact you. This is a tricky situation, but it is terribly important that you involve yourself in any staff appointments that will be made after your appointment. You will need to discuss these appointments with the board chair and understand who has been making staff appointments in the six months before you take on the role. You can ask to review the short-listed applicants' resumes, you can ask to review the resume of the final recommended applicant, you can even ask to be on the selection panel. Whatever the board chair permits, do your darndest to make sure you are comfortable with any new appointment. Whatever appointments are being made, you will be responsible for them.

2. Any issues with staff, the board or parents that you should be aware of. The current head of your new school should declare these to you, and this is another good conversation to have with the board chair. There should be no surprises for you when you take up the role. Toward the end of my principal career, I took up one role as principal where the school and the board had yet to determine if the staff should receive a salary increase in line with all independent schools in the region. This became my first priority, but I could have done without it.

3. Be sure you know the next year's budget. In most principal appointments, you can generally be involved in the budget process. This is yet another request to be made of the board chair, but it is perfectly reasonable for you to know and understand the budget that you will inherit. And if you have concerns, speak up.

In hindsight

There is a significant period between the official announcement and the first day of your new job. This period must be managed well; it is just as important as any other stage in the journey for your wellbeing and reputation, as well as for the colleagues around you.

This can also be a period of mixed emotions and confused feelings. You are keen to engage with your new school, to do things *now* to ensure a smooth transition. But first things first – manage your departure well by helping the school make the necessary arrangements to prepare for the change. Once you have arrangements in place at your current school, you can turn your attention to your new school. While you haven't officially started, you can still be involved in important decisions that will have a direct bearing on you in your new role.

Chapter 2

GAME ON!

THE FIRST HUNDRED DAYS

This phrase – the first hundred days – is often attributed to Franklin D Roosevelt and refers to a prime minister or president's first 100 days in office. This phase is crucial to any leader, and the work you do in this period – your accessibility, availability, interactions, public speaking, newsletter articles, community emails and other writings and activities – set the foundation for your tenure.

The well-known phrase, "Do not adapt to the energy in the room, influence the energy in the room" was my mantra. You are the principal now, act like it.

Meet key people prior to starting

Once you've taken up the job and are sitting in your new office, then you can take a breather and congratulate yourself. You did it!

It is a good idea to have a casual get together with your executive team on a weekend prior to starting. This would usually be arranged for you, but try to keep it informal. Life will be intense once you start your new role, and seeing your key staff in a casual environment prior to starting can be really sustaining. If nothing has been arranged, don't take it personally – organise something yourself.

The ideal time for a principal to start a new role is in January, at the start of a new academic year. Schools can appoint the deputy or an executive leader in an acting capacity until you start. Of course, it isn't always possible and sometimes you will be required to start during the year, but I recall during the first week or so of each of my principalships, when it was still school holidays, I seemed to have much more time on my hands than when in the job proper.

The other observation I would make relates to something that made settling in a challenge: everyone thought I knew everything about everything. I didn't. This is where my executive assistant was gold. I relied on her heavily.

Succeeding in your new position is now your main game. Don't forget, you are the principal! Your community expect you to lead. They will be patient early on, but they expect you to lead.

There are many situations in the independent school system where a principal has not survived their five-year contract because they failed to meet the expectations of their school community. I know of one principal who was terminated under the terms of their contract after three years. This is not uncommon.

In the case of the principal I knew, in the first six months, the school community was keen to meet the new principal. The expectations around the principals performance were low, the community of staff, students and parents just wanted to meet the new principal, to get to know him, who he was, what his values and beliefs were, and the hopes and aspirations he held for the school. The community wanted to see the new principal at events and functions, leading information sessions and sharing his plans for the school. His commitment to being visible and present was not strong.

In the latter half of the first year, the community's expectations changed. Staff and parents wanted to see the principal solving problems, they wanted to meet with the principal and have him hear and address their concerns. Staff were looking to the principal to set the school up for the following year. The board was asking for an annual operational plan for the following year. The principal was expected to develop a strong budget that delivered educational services and programs and addressed the poor academic outcomes for year 12 students.

In this principal's second year the board and the community expected him to perform. The settling in period was over. The board members expected business plans to support necessary change and improvement, they wanted strategy and forward thinking from the principal, they wanted publicly voiced matters of concern addressed, and they wanted the principal to have a plan to address falling enrolments.

This is common – whatever the challenges might be for a new principal in any school, there is an expectation that the principal will perform in their second year. In the second half of the second year, the board in this particular school wanted outcomes. Unbeknown to the principal, the board and executive leaders were informally assessing his performance. The general feeling was that he wasn't up to standard, and the mood changed.

The board put in place a performance plan with key performance targets and areas that the principal had to address, including a timeline and success criteria. They gave him six months to show improvement. He wasn't able to and the board invoked the six-month termination clause in the principal's contract.

If only that principal had stepped up to the plate at the beginning, his community would have supported him to success in the role. In these situations, communication is imperative. I would recommend that, prior to your official start or as early in the piece as possible, you schedule a one-on-one session with each one of your executive leaders. This is more than a get-to-know-you session, this is intelligence gathering. Ask them what projects and initiatives are in the pipeline, what challenges linger from before your start that will need to be addressed, and what should be the immediate priorities for you as the new principal. Of course, spend some time getting to know your new colleagues – ask them how long they have been in their current position, what they enjoy, what challenges them, and how you can support them in their role. It is a good idea to let them know your leading learning intention and to ask them what their professional learning plans are for the year ahead, and how you (as their new principal) can support them.

An impressive start is your rock

In the beginning, everyone will be watching you. The board, parents, staff, students, alumni, businesses run by the school and affiliated businesses, your collegial associations and their individual members, and competitor schools. Everyone will be looking for confirmation that you are a good fit for the position and for the school.

It's important to be deliberate about creating the optimal image right from the beginning of your tenure. Don't forget the leadership identity you created for yourself during the preparation phases and application process – be true to this.

In each role I made it a habit to spend a lot of my time on my feet, walking around and talking to as many people as possible, from all parts of the school. These first interactions establish who you are and what people can expect of you.

You are the principal and as a wise leader you need be clear-eyed about the behaviours you expect. You will see behaviours that you do not accept, or feel are not consistent with the school's ethos. Take your time and think these challenges through but be deliberate about how to change those behaviours when necessary. This starts from your first day. I tried to establish early on that my office would be a well-oiled, professional business centre, with an open-door policy. Everybody could be sure they would be met with a broad smile and warm hello.

I had a colleague whose mantra was that no-one left his office bruised or demoralised. I tried as hard as I could to meet this standard but, given the content of some conversations I had to have, it was not always possible. However, in your first 100 days you can make it a habit. Tongues will wag and people will know that the new boss is a good person.

As a new principal, it's important to listen carefully, ask questions, and engage with your new community. Listen carefully to the directions that your board chair offers and ask other trusted colleagues for suggestions on ways to measure up to your school's expectations.

Develop positive relationships

Once you start your new job, make it a priority to establish positive relationships and gain the trust of your executive team and your colleagues. This will create a very healthy foundation for your future with the school.

You will have several critical relationships to put your energy, effort and time into. I will have a stab at the order in which I think you should prioritise them:

1. Spouse
2. Children
3. Executive assistant (EA)
4. Deputy principal (and I advocate that you *must* have one)
5. Board chair.

After that, work at every relationship.

There were many occasions when I simply could not be in attendance at my school. I might be at meetings of professional bodies, attending to my own professional learning or taking a break – and this was when my deputy would do their best work. In longer term absences such as sabbatical or long-service leave, my deputy would step in to lead and manage the school, maintaining its overall stability and cultural direction.

Why have a deputy?

For me, the most significant benefit of having a good deputy was the support they provided in the leadership of the school and the overall management of staff. My deputy would work closely with me every day to ensure the smooth overall operation of the school.

As principal, I had ultimate responsibility, but it was helpful to me to have a trusted deputy to share the burden.

My deputy would support me to meet the community expectation that I would be at every event. Sharing the role of attending functions with my deputy appeased the community expectation.

My deputy would work on resolving conflicts between various individuals – including students, teachers, parents or a combination – seeing that the conflict didn't escalate to me.

I can't understate the importance of strong relationships with your spouse and children. Any family strain will inevitably make its way to work. Anytime there was a family dispute at home (usually on the stroke of when I was leaving for work), it was hard for me to settle and to be present at work in the calm and even state of mind I needed to be in for staff, students and parents. In the same way, if I showed up at home still carrying tension from work, that could destabilise the calm in my home and unsettle my family. I established an end of day routine to ensure I showed up at home at the end of the day as a father and husband and not a cranky principal.

As soon as possible, establish trust with your EA. You may already have met, but just as likely not. In any case, go out of your way to make clear how much you are looking forward to working together.

Principals can succeed without having a good relationship with their EA – but it's rare and makes life much harder. Your first few meetings together should be useful, professional, and instructional. Try to avoid having others in the room so you can have an honest discussion about what you both want from the relationship.

I made a pact with each of my EAs to agree publicly and disagree privately. Nothing runs round the office more quickly, or more destructively, than the two of us falling out in a room full of people.

Your EA will go over and above what is required, but that is something you shouldn't take for granted. Once, an EA sat with me in a very hostile and threatening meeting with two parents whose children were involved in bullying. The mother was engaged in a seemingly never-ending email conversation with me about the alleged bullying of her children by other students. My preliminary investigations and conversations with staff indicated that the shoe was on the other foot. Her children were indeed the bullies. This was not something I wanted to get involved in, but I knew I had to. I had no choice but to meet with the mother if I wanted to resolve this.

I invited the mother to attend a meeting in my office, with her husband, and I asked my EA to join the meeting to take notes, so I could concentrate on the conversation.

I was extremely anxious, especially when the father started an expletive-laden, threatening, verbal attack on my character. I sat on the edge of my chair, with the father on the opposite side of the coffee table to me. I had positioned myself carefully and was poised to launch myself at him in a rugby-style tackle if he moved out of his seat. I felt sure he was going to get physical with me, but I managed to diffuse the situation, avoid an altercation, and end the meeting with all parties intact. The matter was not resolved. At the end of the day, I had to call on the board and the board chair to terminate the enrolment of the children. The board supported me.

Suffice to say, my diminutive EA didn't find that in her role description, but carried herself with a quiet, calm demeanour throughout.

In all my new jobs, I found that most people were happy to help ensure a smooth transition for me, as the new person on the job. Seek the helpful, supportive people out and maintain regular communication from early on. Avoid complaining to fellow employees. You never know who will quote you or cast you in a negative light. If someone starts complaining or gossiping directly to you, try to stay neutral, if possible. If you can't deflect or switch topics, then ask constructive questions instead.

Develop positive working relationships with staff at all levels of the organisation, with particular emphasis on the people you'll be working with regularly. Forging strong relationships will enhance your overall work performance, work hard on this from the beginning.

Meet with stakeholders to get your view of the school

In the first few weeks, go out of your way to reach out to key stakeholders. These include the chair, of course, the school captains, the president of the parents & friends association (P&F), and the presidents of the alumni association and staff association. Reach out to them by email or a phone call, and set up a meeting.

Arrange to meet the most senior people in the school's community in the first few weeks. This is when you most need their view from outside the office, when you are not yet so committed to your plans that you can't act on what they say.

I remember at Moreton Bay College, a parent met with me in the first month – I thought that was jolly decent of him. He worked in a local bank and told me in quite sinister tones that he had done a financial check on me and knew everything about me. That was back in 1999 – there is certainly no such thing as "private" in the 2020s, with your digital footprint out there for everyone to see.

Meet with as many people as you can. I set up a diary of appointments for my first term, trying to meet with dozens and dozens of parents, staff, and students. At each meeting I would ask them two questions:

1. What must not change?
2. What would you like to see changed?

After the first few weeks, you should become more strategic about stakeholder meetings. They could fill your whole diary, but then you wouldn't have any time to act on what you find out from them. Meet the people who will make or break your key priorities. You've got an executive team and (probably) dozens of middle leaders to gather information from. Think about who will be seeing the things you don't know about yet, and prioritise hearing from them.

A colleague of mine said to me, "I plan on going on a listening tour for the first six months."

I liked that, and quipped, "Will you do some speaking at some stage?" But it is sage advice. Do lots of listening and less talking in the first 100 days.

Impact is everything

Keep a running list of quick hits and bandaids. If you can't manage to maintain a list of what you want to change, ask your EA to do it. If something small can be fixed straight away, do it straight away. Ask your EA or deputy to make a list of the big problems the school faces, and start working on them.

This is the time to make the U-turns that your predecessor couldn't. They may not have been able to admit that an important strategic policy had failed, but you can – and it's better to do so. It happens too often, the predecessor sat on their hands because they knew they were leaving. This also leaves you with a lot of work to do – all those balls in the air have to land.

It's understandable that you'll have a lot to catch up on in a new job and may not have insights and opinions to share right out of the gate. However, sitting silently in meeting after meeting won't make a great impression, either. Instead, aim to strike a balance between listening carefully (which will be extremely important in getting oriented) and speaking up or asking quality questions.

Here are five important lessons that I learned that helped me make a positive impact right from the start:

1. Be genuine
2. Know who you are and what you stand for
3. Be intentional
4. Be considerate
5. Be curious.

Establish open communication channels with your board chair and executive team members, whether this takes the form of weekly meetings or recurring email or text updates. In this digital age, leaders have moved away from phone calls – but a phone call works wonders. Effective communication is about impact on others. The critical importance of communication is discussed at length in chapter 6.

Set the standards you want met

For the first few weeks, your every move – from the coffee you order at the cafeteria to your behaviour in the car park lines – will be scrutinised. It is important to be aware of this scrutiny as your staff, students and parents will be watching you to see if you walk the walk.

If you know how highly visible you are as you move around your school and the wider community, you can prepare for being seen. Give some thought to the details, like how you will dress when shopping at the local supermarket on the weekend. I would always dress one step above the "audience", something my father taught me.

I arrived at Hunter Valley Grammar School in 2006, when the catch cry from parents was, "Why are we paying independent-school fees and getting a state-school education?" This was no disrespect to public education. It was the opposite, a swipe at the quality of education parents were paying for at our school. The grounds, facilities, buildings, and playing fields were neglected and unkempt. There were more bare patches of dirt than turf. And parents were voting with their feet. The physical campus is a learning space too; a well-kept campus creates a positive learning environment for children and young adults and shows them that we (the school) care about and value our surroundings. I found that when the grounds and facilities were well maintained, the children were far more inclined to keep the spaces where they sat and played in good condition.

I knew that if I wanted to turn the place around, I needed my grounds team on side. I despaired one day when I saw a groundsman on top of a Toro Greensmaster drive over paper, cutting it to small pieces and throwing it all over the turf. I knew I had a job on my hands.

But when the (resident) plumber saw me pick up a dozen pieces of paper on my walk from A block to my office, about 25 metres, he was sold. The plumber immediately told the other ground staff; my job to get the grounds team on side was made a whole lot easier by that simple act.

In 2013, in response to a horrible scandal involving sexual misconduct and degradation, chief of the army, Lieutenant-General David Morrison said, "The standard you walk past is the standard you accept." I like to use this with early-career and aspiring principals – in the most holistic way. Kids see this too – they watch you as principal, very keenly. If you have high uniform standards and you walk past a lad wearing his tie at half-mast and his shirt covering his thighs, but you do nothing about it – you lose! If you walk past of group of students and an expletive fills the air, the kids know you heard – what does walking past tell them? If a teacher is on their smart phone while supervising a class, the kids see you but the teacher doesn't, and you don't intervene, what message are you sending?

The first 100 days is also the time to be clear about your management style: how you will treat others and how they should treat you. Being clear on this will save everyone from wasting valuable energy trying to figure out how best to work alongside you. Don't be afraid to set some rules – it's helpful, rather than stiff.

A set of personal dos and don'ts would have helped me. I learned that it's fine to say you don't work on Sundays. It's fine to say you'd like someone to fetch a sandwich at lunchtime. As head of the school, how you use your time is your most important decision.

So get control of your diary. The staff in my schools were keen to get in to see me as soon as possible, they were enthusiastic to share their stories and ideas. I found it hard to find the right balance between being available for staff, which was important, and managing the other competing demands for my time. I worked on my schedule to make sure that my diary was organised around my priorities. In chapter 3 I discuss in more detail about how to find the right balance with time management.

Over my career I found the number of meeting requests for the last week of any term would grow to a crescendo. I was amused how many staff wanted to see me in the last week – clearly, they were clearing the decks before the holidays. I had an agreement with my EA: any such meetings would be met with, "Paul is not available this week, but he is available in the first week of the holidays." Unbelievable how few requests made it to week one of the holidays.

Above all, decide how you are going to behave on the bad days – and you are certainly going to have them – when it all goes pear-shaped. On such days you will probably feel both worried and, particularly if your team has screwed up, very cross. Keep your cool. Not only will it help get people focused on getting out of the hole, but it will mark you out as a principal to be respected and supported. There will always be time for the inquest a bit further down the track.

Your work ethic

Let people see you working hard, with a strong work ethic. Let it be known from your actions and words that you are fully accountable, you accept responsibility for the lot.

Never, ever utter, "I don't have enough time." There is never enough time, so manage people's expectations of how much of your time you will give them. In the first 100 days, as you set your standard, make sure you always have enough time for the important things that can make a huge difference for staff, students and parents. Let them know you will do anything for them, and you have their backs no matter what. Make it clear that you welcome challenges, criticism, and viewpoints other than your own.

If you do need to vent at work, consider taking your deputy, or another trusted colleague, into your confidence. But be mindful of the potential consequences should your trust be broken. I found that debriefing with family and friends was a good outlet as well. Seeking professional help when things get tough is also a good idea. Schools have employee assistance programs (EAPs) – voluntary, employer-sponsored programs that help employees navigate stressful life circumstances. EAPs are usually free for the participating employee to use.

Endeavor to arrive earlier and/or stay later than most staff. The facilities manager and grounds team will probably beat you to work, but be there before teachers and your executive team. Show them that you are ready to work hard.

The new generation of principals and CEOs are starting from a different base than I did. In a welcome change to approach, they seem more committed to overtly showing that family commitments are important. They are more explicit about this, and they are more prepared to work remotely and approve the same of their executive leaders, promoting flexible work arrangements. COVID-19 has meant that flexible work arrangements are far more acceptable than in my career as a principal and CEO. These are positive changes to the paradigm of the independent school principal.

Lead yourself

Chapter 3 discusses this critical aspect of who you are as a leader in more depth, but I touch on the concept of "leading yourself" here as it pertains to how you start your new role.

Identify potential mentors within your organisation and get to know them. Depending on the capability of your chair, they should be able to fill this role. In a recent position the board chair did this very well. It made a huge difference to how effective I could be. I have benefitted in all my roles from a chair who wanted me to be successful and took a genuine personal and professional interest in me. If this is not happening for you, cultivate it.

Solicit feedback from your executive team periodically in the first 100 days and respond positively to constructive criticism. Make it clear to your chair and other staff that you are all about a learning journey. Just note, as a new principal you have much to learn, and that is OK.

In the early days, your on-the-job learning is best done through informal, casual conversations, rather than in writing. I would be surprised that anyone would dare commit to writing what they thought about the new boss in the first 100 days.

Create a professional development plan with clear goals and objectives outlining what you will learn and the skills you will acquire. Consult the chair, executive leaders, or professionals in your field and find out what certifications, coursework, and/or degrees would be most effective at advancing your career.

Spend time with your key executive colleagues, not just in formal, minuted meetings. A regular dinner with the two or three most important can help and act as an early-warning system.

And see the chair often enough. You won't be able to do much without them. By the end of your first 100 days, the parents, the staff and the students should understand what you are trying to do with their school. You should have provided a frame through which they interpret the activities of the school. If you don't provide such a frame, someone else will – and it will not be the one you want.

Some professional development resources

There are range of organisations in Australia and abroad who can assist you develop yourself as a leader. The associations that I used to support my professional development were:

- AHISA https://ahisa.edu.au/
- AIS NSW https://www.aisnsw.edu.au/ (in particular their Leadership Centre's Principal Induction Program for early career principals)
- ACEL https://www.acel.org.au/ACEL/
- AITSL https://www.aitsl.edu.au/
- AIM https://www.aim.com.au/

These are all in the education space and not-for-profit organisations.

In hindsight

No first 100 days are the same for any principal. And you can never prepare for the unanticipated outcomes.

A colleague shared with me his graphic representation of leadership, and I found it most apt for new principals as they learn their trade.

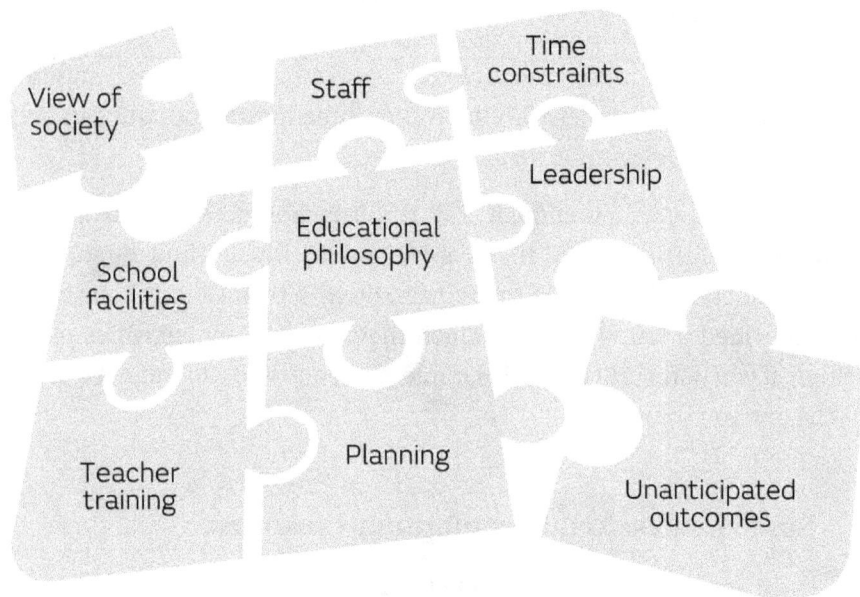

While every principalship is highly contextual and the first days for principals will be different depending on the school's context, I have been struck when chatting to colleagues by how much common ground there is.

Reach out to your colleagues in the early days. Relationships matter! Positive professional relationships can make most organisational structures work. Those relationships are set in the first 100 days. For many, they pass in a blur of activity, and sometimes crisis. But it is my belief, born of experience, that those who invest in managing that first period in office will reap the rewards.

THE HONEYMOON IS OVER

The time will come when the gloss wears off. The community was patient and tolerant with you as you settled in, then the atmosphere changes. The demands and expectations for change will come.

After the first 100 days, it's time to knuckle down and start working on the skills you will need to sustain success in the new role.

Reflecting on the first year of my first role as principal – way back at Moreton Bay College in 1999, when I was bright eyed and bushy tailed – I can recognise some of the core skills I would have benefitted from:

- Dealing with conflict amongst the team
- Influencing and motivating the team
- Handling performance reviews and remedial actions
- Finding resources needed to support the team
- Finding the next generation of leaders and supporting career paths for them
- Learning how to deal with the basics of personal and (my office's) organisational capacity.

One of the best ways to develop yourself, as an aspirant, is to ask your current principal for opportunities to learn and practice these skills.

What do you focus on after the first 100 days?

If I could go back and give myself some advice at the time of my new appointments, I would tell myself the below. I have found that my mentees are better at taking my advice than I am myself!

First, take a deep breath
You will now be viewing things from a different perspective. Take a breath. Your decisions need to be deliberate. Change for change's sake rarely works. You will be judged by your community every day; that remains consistent. They will become less tolerant; they will expect you to lead and manage. Making mistakes after the settling-in period is not a good way to develop confidence among your team members. Be deliberate and purposeful, take your time to make good decisions.

Avoid the temptation to micro-manage
It's important that you don't micro-manage others. You are equipped with new knowledge, deeper understanding, more information – but don't make the mistake of believing you can do

things better than anyone else, and avoid the instinct to step in and do the job yourself.

Avoid the superhero complex. Because you know the job, it's easy to jump in and save the day. This short-term success may inhibit long-term success. Part of your job as principal is to teach others to do things better and to develop strategies to improve the performance of others.

I have seen some principals go the other way – they delegate everything and want to sit in their office and ponder the future. It's equally important you don't remove yourself altogether from the decision making that you have delegated. This is a quick way to lose touch. You need to be involved in the process to see where improvements can be made. To ensure things stay on track, touch base regularly with your key staff and develop good processes. I connected with my executive leaders through regular one-on-ones. In those meetings I would make sure that my executives understood how their work contributed to the bigger picture. I would draw a clear line between a task or project and the broader school goal it supported.

The best way I found for keeping engagement high was to check on my team's motivation levels at our meetings, casual check-ins, during one-on-ones, or at any time in between.

I tried to create an environment where my leaders had a strong sense of purpose, opportunities to master their craft, and the autonomy to make day-to-day decisions about their work.

Never stop listening
Listening is one of the most important skills you can have. How well you listen has a major impact on the effectiveness of your leadership and on the quality of the relationships you will have with others. I listen so that I hear what people are really saying; to obtain information; to understand; to make people feel valued; and, most importantly, to learn.

A colleague used the term "emergent listening" (Davies, 2014), a skill and practice she developed over her time as a principal. Davies uses the practice when talking and listening to children. However, it is a valuable practice for leaders and principals to consider.

I know from ad nauseum conversations that it is common when listening to fit what we hear into what we already know. When practising emergent listening I like to begin with what is known (Davies, 2014), and open myself up to wanting to learn something new. By not constraining myself to my own beliefs, thoughts and knowledge, I move towards new knowledge and understandings. In doing so, I introduce curiosity to the conversation.

Listening generally means you just take in information and head for a solution; with emergent listening you can go beyond that. When you purposefully put yourself in someone else's shoes, you can dig deeper into their ideas and unpack them more fully. This kind of listening is essential for conducting interviews, fostering collaboration with colleagues, and connecting one-on-one with your team about their personal and professional development.

Continue to walk the walk

Now that you are more familiar with the role and the community, and you have been delegated authority, your community will take their cues from you. For example, if you expect everyone to show up on time for meetings, you need to make sure you are there on time as well. It took me forever to set this norm at one of my schools. I couldn't understand why a scheduled meeting never started on time - people would drift in when it suited. I learned that my predecessor was never on time and had to be chased around the school by his EA (my EA also) to get him to a meeting. It was so entrenched in the school that it took me my first year to change this. In hindsight, I should have worked more stridently at it - like all things that must change, get stuck into it, don't put it off.

Celebrate successes

This is more important than I ever understood or paid proper attention to. Make sure you take the time to celebrate successes along the way. Don't take credit for the success personally. Give credit where credit is due. When the team wins, you win. People in your community will be working hard for you and the school; they will be doing their bit to support you. In most cases, you won't even know it. Do offer public praise so that others see you acknowledge success. This also demonstrates what you define as extraordinary and helps others to model this behaviour. On the other hand, if you must discipline or counsel team members, do it privately to avoid embarrassing them in front of their peers.

Build relationships

Chapter 4 will deal with this more deeply. I don't want this to sound repetitive, but it is one of the most important takeaways. Every month you are in the role – until you retire gracefully to your beach house, or to your Barrington Tops farm overlooking the beautiful Hunter Valley in NSW – this will be so important and will demand your energy, effort and time.

Now you are the principal, you don't have friends (in your workplace), but you can still be friendly. Building rapport and demonstrating that you genuinely care about your team are essential. However, don't seek personal relationships from your school community – this is fraught with risk. Keep your friends outside of the school, they are going to be important to you on many levels. You will compromise your leadership, at some stage, if you have friends within the community.

I found that I was at my best when I was managing relationships well. There is no substitute for building and nurturing relationships with all in your community. It is a fundamental pillar of leadership and will be important in the first 100 days and for all time.

Get to know everyone you can; learn people's names, especially staff. This is very hard – seasoned principals have their own ways of going about it. I found it hard to get to know students by name, as a principal. I would closely observe who was receiving recognition at assemblies, who was giving reports, who was performing. I would make mention of them and repeat their name repeatedly, trying to make a tangible connection or association with their name. I would make notes after the assembly.

In a similar vein, I had the capacity to spot the children who seemed to stay "under the radar," who didn't stand out. I would always enquire about them of their teacher, and then I sought them out to have a chat. This helped me learn their names and more about them.

Another useful tool was to keep a book of each child's individual photo on my desk. These are easy to generate and most school photographers provide them as part of their offering. I took every opportunity to learn a name, and then I practised. When I went on school camp, I took the year level photo book with me. I would hear the name of a student mentioned, look them up in the photo book and get that ah-ha moment when I recognised the face immediately. Usually it would be the kid horsing around in the playground.

When you build relationships, in those unplanned and informal chats, talk about your family and hobbies so your human side travels with you. Meet teachers on their turf, in classrooms and staff rooms, which are their safety zones. Search out teachers who are less vocal, and respect those known to be less than supportive. Again, listen. It is the way your staff will feel valued.

A close colleague of mine, who led a school of over 2000 students and 500 staff, told me during my case study research that he tried to know five things about each staff member. He felt if he could show that he knew five things then he would win their respect and support. He recalled how he saw a teacher at a local restaurant, this then became the starting point for a conversation. This practice could also be used by teachers with their students, so that the student understands their teacher cares and is interested in them as a person.

Get to know past students, the bus drivers, cafeteria staff (if you want a good coffee this is imperative), non-teaching staff, and the parents who lead the support organisations. I nurtured my relationship with the cafeteria manager, Andrew, and eventually he even let me choose the coffee bean.

Extend your relationship building to your principal colleagues in other schools, making your own region a priority. In my first year, I ensured I was completely committed to our associations, I volunteered for roles and the odd task that had to be done. Your colleagues can be your best mentors as you learn about and adjust to the culture of your region. And you'll need to have the executive officers of the professional associations as partners when, not if, you need them. When advocacy is needed, it's invaluable to have friends in other schools and the offices of the peak bodies.

Each person with whom you work has a personal story, family, and dreams. Tap into that. Share some of your own dreams. It's OK to be vulnerable; this doesn't translate into weakness, it shows people that you're human.

Honour staff

After six months, I made direct steps to break down the divide between teachers and non-teachers that seems to beset schools. It has been a feature in all schools I have worked in, and I made it my legacy that when I left, there would be one staff.

My late father wore it as his badge that he had a raised a good man because I knew the gardener as well as I knew my deputy.

Teachers, especially, will be watching you. It was a funny thing, but I found the non-teachers to be more supportive, less judgemental, and more philanthropic than the teachers. I risk being criticised for saying this, but throughout my career teachers were a lot harder work than non-teachers when it came to cultural alignment and support for the long-term view of the school.

Some staff have seen leaders come and go and will try to wait you out, knowing that each new leader brings some new reform through the revolving door. I have seen this happen, and in most schools I have had to act relatively swiftly on under-performance from a long-serving staff member – some of whom seemed to have been a protected species under my predecessor.

As mentioned earlier, asking teachers "What must not change" and "What would you like to see changed" should ferret out their real concerns and show from the beginning that you value and need their insights. Take notes and check that you're understanding. Probe for deeper meanings.

At a staff meeting in the second half of the year, present an aggregation of these conversations. Use it to tell staff, "This is what I heard you saying. Does it resonate with you?" Rich discussions will follow. Again, genuine listening to both the verbal and nonverbal elements in the conversation is crucial. This will truly be a faculty meeting because the agenda comes from their concerns and hopes.

The collective wisdom of your staff is invaluable. Tap into it respectfully, and teachers will see that you're eager to learn from them and that you honour their expertise. This is best done after the settling in period, and after you have survived the first 100 days.

The second half of the year is a really good time to pull your parents together. Prepare for a very significant parent evening. Some principals like to do this early in the piece, I recommend waiting until you have a stronger sense of the school culture and parent expectations.

The parent evening can be a (professional) warts and all. Be sure to have drinks and canapes (the ones you can eat comfortably without the content of the hors d'oeuvres running all over your hand), have all the staff and directors there, and make everyone feel welcome to your school. Share matter and substance with your parents that they will feel really privileged to receive. I would always include:

- What it is to be an independent school: governance, funding, and autonomy
- A high-level analysis of the budget, just the big-ticket items so parents could see major income and expenditure
- Previous year 12 results and destinations
- Broad curricula
- Clear, distinct, and unequivocal points of difference to key competitors
- Major goals and plans for the next twelve months
- What I expected of parents
- Anything else that ensured I ingratiated myself to parents.

Don't let anyone else speak! It is your night. There will be other occasions when other staff will speak. If you have called the information evening, be sure to deliver.

Pick your battles

As a leader, you will have to pick some battles. Some you must win, others you will have to concede defeat. Always act graciously, bearing in mind the skills of communication and relationship building we have already discussed.

Chewing gum was forbidden in one school when I arrived as principal, but it was everywhere – a disgrace! I stepped in. I asked for teachers to keep lists of "chewers", and after the second offense, they reported the student to me; yes, me. Parents were called if the chewing continued. If you have a code of conduct or a behaviour management framework that includes certain rules, it is important that the consequences for breaches are applied and that all staff get behind enforcement of the code. If these matters are not addressed effectively, children will quickly learn they are negotiable or optional.

Some battles can never be won. Recognise these and set them aside. Consistent resistance from your loyal senior student leaders or your faithful executive leader colleagues will let you know when a battle is not worth fighting.

At one school, I wanted to end an agreement with a counselling service provider; I was not satisfied with the work being done by this person. My deputy told me it was not a battle worth fighting. This turned out to be an astute piece of advice – my deputy understood that there were bigger issues that I needed to attend to.

Other battles are not worth winning or losing. Zero in on those issues that directly affect teaching and learning. Where you spend your time is where your values lie. Or that is how your teachers and your community will interpret what your values are.

When I arrived at one of my new schools, I observed more students out of class than in class. In fact, the behaviour of students in and out of class, and roaming around during class, resembled a zoo. I went to work on this in the second half of my first year and saw visible improvements in my second year.

Initially, I made sure that I was highly visible around the school during lesson times. I engaged with the students who were out of class, keeping the interactions friendly and chatty. I made a point of letting the teacher know that the student was out of class, and asked the teacher to ensure that students did not leave class unless it was critically important.

I had meetings with the faculty (department) heads and we designed a simple system where students had to carry a business card style approval to leave class. We knew this would only have to be a temporary measure while we affirmed that students could not leave class during lessons, save for going to the toilet or sick bay. We got the change we wanted by applying energy and effort to the matter.

Be prepared to back yourself up if you threaten a consequence. I was at a school that celebrated every milestone, including a year 10 dinner dance, which we hosted at school. It was a great event, beautifully organised by the senior staff, who put a lot of heart and soul into ensuring that our students would have a great night.

However, a sub-cultural curse had developed in parallel, with the students organising large before-dance and post-dance parties. The after party became the event. I was new to the position, and when the history was brought to my notice, I warned the students that if I got wind of an after party, I would cancel their dance. Well, it happened. I heard of a party, and I cancelled the dance. On reflection I did wonder if I had made a good or bad decision. Of course, the students were disappointed, but my decision certainly changed the culture of pre-arranged, large gatherings. And the community realised I was a leader who would be true to my word. So, in all, I believe it was good decision.

Delegate

I can't remember how many times in my career I said, "I'll take care of it." In my early days, I walked about the schools with a small A5 journal. More recently I walk the halls and grounds with my iPhone, notes open and the camera ready to capture any matters I need to remember or share.

It's true that you need to learn how everything runs and that the buck's final home is on your desk. But learning to delegate responsibility is the mark of mature leadership. In the first 100 days, it is best to work through as much as you can. But after the honeymoon is over, delegate:

- Separate jobs into "mine", "yours", and "ours" with your EA and deputy. Let them take the ball and run with it, keeping you updated.
- Assure teachers they can manage most discipline issues themselves, but you will happily support them.
- Make sure parents have spoken with teachers before they storm through your office door. Be sure your EA is a gatekeeper. Let parents know that any classroom-related problem must ultimately be solved with the teacher, so it's best to start there. However, trust your instincts. Some complaints belong in your office immediately
- Let your staff manage their own spheres of responsibility, staying close enough that they are comfortable to use you as a reference and a resource

- In the second half of the year, a few board meetings in, feel free to ask directors with unique skills and experience to support you, if it is appropriate.

Trust your instincts. There are times when your accumulated knowledge and wisdom will point you in a certain direction. There are other times when you will have a nagging feeling that a situation needs your direct involvement. You should probably pay attention to that nagging feeling, your instinct or intuition.

In hindsight

I can't find the author of this fable that has done the rounds with principals for many years. A colleague of mine shared this with me when he heard I was writing a book about principalship. I provide it here for some light relief, but it does cut close to the bone.

The story of three envelopes is a business classic for dysfunctional organisations. It starts with an incoming manager replacing a recently fired outgoing manager. On his way out, the outgoing manager hands the new manager three envelopes and remarks, "When things get tough, open these one at a time."

About three months goes by and things start to get rough. The manager opens his drawer where he keeps the three envelopes and opens #1. It reads, "Blame your predecessor." So, he does, and it works like a charm.

Another three months pass and things are growing difficult again, so the manager figures it's time to try #2. It reads, "Restructure." Again, his predecessor's advice works like magic.

Finally, about nine months into the new job, things are getting really sticky. The manager figures it worked before, why not try again. So, he opens the envelope drawer one last time and opens #3. It reads... "Prepare three envelopes."

The moral of this story is – you are the principal, it is your job to lead, accept full responsibility for that.

DIVE INTO THE CULTURE EARLY

Learn the Culture

You will hear principals refer to culture regularly. I like to think of culture as the organisational culture (Schein, 2004); it is the way things are done in your school – a shared sense of purpose and vision; social behaviours and the way people interact with each other; norms; ceremonies; people and relationships; architecture, symbols and artefacts; and identity and image. Climate and culture are interchangeable in my view.

As the new principal you must become the student of that culture, learning how things are done around here. Culture is not the car park gossip! In fact, this is the ante-culture.

Culture is evident in the behaviours you witness – what do teachers do at the end of the day? Do they slip out before the buses have finished loading students, or do they hang around helping kids? How does the school celebrate holidays and staff birthdays? Are kids forbidden to step foot in staff offices and workrooms, or are they welcomed? How are new teachers and students inducted into the school? Assemblies and graduations, January induction and professional development days will all have rules governing how they are run, when they happen, and who does what. Notice the patterns and become part of the culture.

Honour school culture whenever possible, even if it doesn't match your style.

> *When a flower doesn't bloom you fix the environment in which it grows, not the flower. (Heijer, 2019)*

Hunter Valley Grammar School (HVGS) had many community spirit days, including out-of-uniform days, Jeans for Genes Day and footy colours days. Join in! I loved wearing QLD maroon colours on the day of the State of Origin to provoke NSW supporters.

It is your job to sustain, shape, modify, or even overhaul the culture in the school, depending upon what you find. If a toxic school culture is part of your inheritance, you'll need to gradually change it. Such a culture is poison. Teachers may come to dislike one another, gossip may substitute for communication, and discipline can become a power game in which both kids and teachers lose. It will be your job to restore the school to health.

In one of my schools, I walked into a culture of complete mistrust and what seemed like irreparably damaged confidence in the executive leadership and governance of the school. Staff morale was so low it was hard to see how it could be improved. I was told that there was significant trauma amongst staff and the community. Parent trust and confidence was even more damaged. What sort of culture did I find? Demoralisation!

What did I do? Well, the first step was to slowly rebuild trust, which was easier said than done. I concentrated on a few things:

- I made myself available and accessible, and ramped up open and honest communications with all in the community
- I put time, energy and effort into people. Not in grandiose ways, but with lots of one-to-one conversations and the occasional all staff/parent gathering, where I was candid, transparent and sincere
- I focused on my character and my integrity. I treated everyone with the highest esteem, even if I thought they didn't deserve it and even when I knew they offered nothing for me
- I treated staff and parents like they could make a difference
- I accepted responsibility for what I had inherited and took on the responsibility to fix it
- I established a sense of safety and security
- And I led. This meant I accepted responsibility; I took initiative and was open to new ideas; I set an example for learning in self and others; I provided clear direction; I fostered a sense of connection.

At the end of that year, I felt that I had regained the trust and confidence of the parent body, who felt much better about the school's leadership and governance. I didn't win everyone over though – some people held onto the past and found it hard to put trust in new leadership. The same applied to the staff – many were happy, some were not.

I know that the well-worn saying, "You can't see the forest for the trees" applied to me on many occasions. And in the middle of my work at this particular school it was true. I am guilty of sometimes not seeing situations as they really are while I am in the midst of them – I can get too heavily invested in a particular response or attempt to fix something.

I was often pulled out of this by an unexpected email from a parent, affirming my leadership and acknowledging the difference I was making. Emails like this are uplifting.

Dear Paul,

Thanks for the email below and for the level of communication and transparency you've provided since commencing in the role. We haven't met yet, however our son Dominic is in Class 4, but I've appreciated the detail and openness with your communication during a challenging period.

Have a great weekend, Shane.

School culture indicators

There are plenty of signs that your school has a healthy culture:

- While students learn in classrooms, there is also much that is learned implicitly outside of the classroom in a school day
- Lots of support and challenge for individuals in a nurturing environment, there is opportunity for growth for each student and member of staff
- Staff and students (and parents) are encouraged to be engaged and invested in the school
- There is an unmistakable commitment to lifelong learning
- The whole school is a warm, open and generous environment.

There are also signs that things aren't going well:

- There is a lack of a clear sense of shared purpose
- Staff are cold and guarded; conflict is evident
- There is a lack of commitment to learning, development and growth
- A generally negative attitude to student achievement permeates conversations
- There is a lack of faith and confidence in new ideas; low aspirations are evident
- Collaboration is avoided and staff work in silos.

Changing the culture of a school is a long, hard process. But what you, as new principal, own entirely is your own integrity and your ability to listen. Sincere care about those with whom you work, coupled with open and frequent communication, are essential building blocks to a healthy culture. Be patient. Neither Rome nor a healthy school culture were built in a day!

Don't change everything at once

I arrived at Hunter Valley Grammar School (HVGS) in February, just in time to witness my first swim carnival. I couldn't believe it; it was like muck-up day. It did not resemble any swimming carnival I knew from schools and associations I had been involved with previously.

I was shocked but didn't react. I observed what was going on, and in the months that followed I had many casual chats with the director of sport about why. I grew to understand that without novelty, kids wouldn't participate. Slowly, over the subsequent years, the director of sport and I changed the carnivals. Novelty was still evident, but together we introduced an atmosphere of professionalism too. We struck the right balance between raw fun and discipline. The director of sport was a willing ally, he just needed the support from me to make the changes he wanted to make. He understood the school's context and knew that moving to a more traditional, competitive carnival program would not work, but there was a point he could move to to satisfy the needs of the fair-dinkum swimmers as well as those who wanted a fun day out.

In your first months, change absolutely nothing that isn't essential or directed by your school board, except the pictures on your office wall. You're the new kid and learning is your first agenda. Grand visions of turning around a school are noble and possibly necessary, but such change should not be the priority.

I remember how a colleague arranged for some funds and bought a new couch to replace a ramshackle plaid sofa in the principal's office. "Wow," she thought, "They'll love it." She was wrong. The teachers mourned the loss of a piece of furniture that had seen them through so much. I've heard similar stories with unhappy endings, even one in which people griped because the principal replaced drinks in the vending machine with sugar-free versions.

The most unlikely corners of a school's culture can have symbolic value. A new leader may act out of good will yet have difficulty repairing inadvertent damage.

Improving things is, of course, a large part of the principal's agenda. However, before you dive into the waters of change, make sure you know where the rocks are and which sharks lurk close to the surface.

I remember my first winter at an all-girls school in Brisbane. The girls were wearing gloves as part of their uniform. Winter in Brisbane rarely had daytime temperatures below 20 degrees, and it was 1999. Gloves were probably ok in 1929, but not now. I set about retiring the gloves, a decision warmly received by the girls and the staff, but not by the alumni. Wow, did I underestimate the swiftness and toxicity of the response from those adherents to tradition. I was left wondering if I had made a good or bad decision. My barometer was always what is best for the students. So, yes, it was a good decision, even though at the time it caused me significant grief.

Holly Ransom – CEO of disruptive strategy company, Emergent – put it perfectly in a presentation she gave to the staff at one of my schools:

> *"We cannot afford not to be changing. Disruption presents a choice between opportunity and adolescence."*

In my words, grow up, and lead.

Let your community know you are committed

Former principals rule long after their tenures have ended. Behind you stands a long line of predecessors – and their legacies will continue to influence the school community.

Your job is to build a school that becomes a community of educators, dedicated to meeting the needs of students. This can take a long time. In my experience it took three-to-five years before I could see impactful, long-term change.

One good way to announce your commitment and your leadership intent is to set longer-term goals. How does a new principal or CEO set goals when new to the role?

- Before I started the process, I made sure that I understood the school's financial trajectory and that I knew who I wanted on the goal setting "bus"
- If you're unsure of where to start, consider identifying where you'd like to be in five years. Take that information and consider where you'd like to be within one year. Then start thinking about specific goals that you know can be achieved. I tried to set goals that were performance driven, improved outcomes for students, and could be measured
- I like to use an initial SWOT analysis to identify strengths, weaknesses, opportunities, and threats. I would then set goals based on how each could be used to my advantage. Doing the analysis first will help you think through your strategic challenges and opportunities before trying to set targets.
- Gaining insight from employees is a smart strategy, as it will give you perspective from those at the coalface, so to speak. I would ask fellow executives to get involved and support the goals I had set. Once we were on the same page, I would ask the board to endorse my goals and plans. If you do ask for input, be open to actually using it – otherwise employees will be less likely to offer up their opinions in the future
- Do external benchmarking. Have a look and see what your competitors are offering and producing. This information will be helpful to provide ideas that might not have emerged from your SWOT
- Review your past performance. Without knowing where you've come from, it's hard to decide where you should be heading. Past performance can help inform your goals.

Good schools cannot be built quickly. The work of building a good school is an endless journey. But if you put in the time, you'll have the opportunity to positively affect the hearts and lives of many people. You'll be remembered for your honesty, care, and passion for learning. That makes a difference.

One of the very first things I did when I was appointed to HVGS, was to buy a house in the area and let people know that I was staying. And stay I did, for fifteen years. The community drew a sigh of relief because, according to the locals, two of three former principals used their appointment as a stepping stone to bigger and better jobs. To use your first principalship as a stepping stone is to do a disservice to the profession, your teachers, and your students.

Today there is some tension in schools where boards, especially those with a strong corporate version of governance, want a shorter tenure for their CEO/principal. It is relatively normal in the corporate world to change CEOs every few years. This is at odds with what staff in independent schools want and need – to know that the principal is committed.

In hindsight

Former principals rule long after their tenures have ended. Behind you stands a long line of predecessors – and their legacies will continue to influence the school community.

Tips for the first three-to-six months

Reflecting on my first three-to-six months in new roles, I would offer these tips to newly appointed principals as you move out of first gear and into second gear:

- Develop good processes for decision making, meetings, communications and feedback. Set up good routines, give clear messages to your community that you are organised, efficient, steady and sur.
- Tune into the culture of the school when you begin your new job, listen, ask, and observe before acting on issues, and then act. Failing in cultural leadership (Trice and Beyer, 1991) will become an Achilles heel
- Spent time ensuring you make good quality, considered decisions around change. You need to learn, understand and master change leadership (Fullan, 2011)
- Get to know your staff well and in a short timeframe. Any investment in staff in the formative days will bring return after return. Building your social and political capital is a must
- Build keen, mutually beneficial partnerships and networks. This is time consuming work, but it pays.

A DAY IN THE LIFE

It is important for aspiring principals and early career principals to have a clear image of what the job looks like every day. I will tell you this, there are usually no two days alike. And when you think you have planned out a perfect day, expect it to be disrupted with the unexpected.

My days would usually start at 5:00am at the latest. And they wouldn't usually conclude until around 9:00pm. In addition, principals in Australian independent schools can have school commitments two or three nights a week and on the weekend. That is the life!

There are huge demands on your time.

Part of my daily routine had to be a commitment to my own wellbeing, it was necessary to avoid burnout.

My early morning routine would include any combination of exercise, reflection, quiet reading, writing or listening to a podcast.

By around 6:30am I would find myself checking overnight email activity to clear the decks before having breakfast – an absolute must – and getting ready to go to the office. I made a conscientious effort to be in the office by 7:30am every day.

I copied a day from my diary to share what it often really looked like – this does not capture what is done before 7:30am.

TUESDAY 5 FEBRUARY 2019

7:30am –   walk around with the facilities manager to evaluate the state of the grounds and identify projects

8:00am –   board finance sub-committee meeting

8:50am –   speak to year 12 about the year ahead, how they are personally accountable

9:00am –   debrief the finance sub-committee meeting with the chief financial officer

9:30am –   interview for a new non-teaching appointment

10:30am – second interview for the above

11:30am – weekly meeting with the communications team (marketing manager, communications manager, enrolments office, and alumni manager)

12:30pm – fortnightly meeting with the school captains, vice captains and president of Leo Club, the youth organisation of Lions Clubs International.

1:00pm – parent meeting to discuss outstanding debt on school fees and payment plan to sustain a child's enrolment

1:30pm – weekly meeting with the deputy

2:30pm – meeting with local council traffic officers to discuss parking and traffic flow problems in local streets

3:15pm – take a phone call from a fellow principal about a critical matter in their school they want advice on

3:45pm – walk around the classrooms observing the after-school activity and checking on the start of the academic tutoring program

4:15pm – phone call to the board chair to discuss possible termination of a student enrolment due to inappropriate cyber behaviours

4:45pm – board risk & compliance committee meeting

6:00pm – take a break

7:00pm – parent information evening

At HVGS I had a community of more than 3000 who expected to have access to me on any given day. I was complicit in that; I gave them access and wanted them to contact me.

When I was at Moreton Bay College, the job was 7 days a week. Monday to Friday was at school, Saturdays were for Queensland Girls Secondary Schools Sports Association (QGSSSA) sport and Sundays required me to attend the local Uniting Church.

Because the week is so full of appointments and scheduled commitments, it is nigh impossible to find time for the big picture thinking that is required in the job. So your weekends, and/or the student vacation periods, become your thinking time. I worked every weekend because my in-tray and my to-do list had to be cleared before I could start a new week. The weekend I would spend writing an assembly speech, a newsletter item or a submission for the board. I know many of my colleagues had a routine of Saturday sporting commitments and Sunday church.

My days were appointments, appointments, commitments and commitments! There were days when I could have fifteen face-to-face appointments, this is no exaggeration. Some days I didn't find time to eat. At the end of those days, I was exhausted. It was little wonder why.

It was not daily, but at some point during the week I would usually be required to give my attention to the state based AIS, teacher unions, community services, children's guardian and other like agencies, local police, and the hierarchy of the affiliated churches. Committing to these groups was generally non-delegable.

Most days I would have to invest time in managing the complex family relationships around the students – split families, blended families, complex marriages, and access/settlement arguments. More recently issues around gender identity have arisen in schools, creating new challenges for schools and principals.

Board meetings

Board meetings usually occur twice a term, and despite the seeming infrequency of them, they always loomed larger than life and occupied a lot of my time. The board meeting required significant preparation and there were always follow-up actions.

Aspirants have asked me what a board meeting looks like and what you are required to do at a board meeting. The business of a board meeting is highly contextual. Here is a typical board agenda that you would find in most independent schools:

- Welcome, introduction and opening remarks from the chair, which includes conflict of interest declarations
- Record of attendees, apologies, and correspondence
- Approval of the previous minutes. Particular directors can be pedantic about the accuracy of minutes
- Business arising from the previous minutes. Principals are usually set a range of actions or tasks that require action and reporting to the next board meeting
- Board subcommittee reports, which will most surely comprise the finance report. The monthly financial statements are a terribly

important part of any agenda. The reports are usually presented by the chair of the finance subcommittee

- Principal's report. This will be discussed in detail in chapter 5
- Other business. This will also be discussed in chapter 5. This is where the surprises can happen. Expect to break out in a cold sweat when a director drops something on the table that blindsides you.

How to manage the load

The job of principal can wear you down if you don't get the work-life balance right. It can dominate your life if you let it. Take measures early on to see that this doesn't happen. The expectation of long days and self-sacrifice may be shifting with the new generation of principals and CEOs; I hope so.

I did have a good work/life balance, but I only got there after experience in the role.

The best preparation for the daily load is to start now, wherever you are at on your pathway to principalship. Develop good habits, routines, rituals and discipline, and jettison distractors. Start to build the skills and practices that you will rely on when you are in the arena. If you can't manage now, enlist the help of a top-shelf lifestyle coach.

You will work 10-hour days at least. Here is my list of the top twelve things to do to help you manage your daily load:

1. Make time for your personal well-being – that means allocating time for health, fitness, and rest
2. Your best and most enduring work is done face-to-face – it takes up a lot of time, but it saves a lot of time too
3. Avoid the lure of email – email interrupts work, extends the workday, intrudes on time for family and thinking, and is not conducive to thoughtful discussions. Tell your staff that you don't want to be copied in on FYI emails
4. Be agenda driven – a clear and effective agenda optimises your limited time; without one, demands from the loudest constituencies will take over, and the most important work won't get done

5. Limit your routine responsibilities – examine every activity that falls into the routine and have-to-do categories. Does it serve an important purpose? If not, remove it

6. Rely on your direct reports – the more you can delegate to your leadership team, the better you will generally feel about your use of time.

7. Avoid meetings – regularly review which meetings are truly needed and which can be delegated, and let go of meetings that seemed idiosyncratic of the previous principal. Take a hard look at meeting length. I had a default length of 30 minutes.

8. Allow for accessibility and spontaneity – these enhance your legitimacy. Leaders whose schedules are always booked up, or whose EAs say no to too many people, risk being viewed as imperious, self-important or out of touch. EAs play a key role in finding the right balance here.

9. Carve out alone time – it's vital that you schedule adequate uninterrupted time by yourself so that you can have space to reflect and prepare for meetings.

10. Juggle external constituencies – everyone wants to talk to you and dealing with external stakeholders is time-consuming. It often involves longer workdays and time away from headquarters and from home. Keep them in check!

11. Find time for parents, they are the customers of your school – most principals just don't spend enough time with them. Five minutes with a parent on the phone can save you 30–60 minutes in an email exchange.

12. Limit time with directors – encourage them to bring business to the board table.

In hindsight

You will have a heavy workload – the amount of stuff you have to deal with in one day will push the boundaries of what can realistically be done. The heavy workload comes from the sheer volume of work that needs to be done, and the load can seem much heavier than it is if you do not have good organisational skills to manage your work. One important means to manage the load is through delegation.

The ability to delegate is one of the hallmarks of a successful leader. While effective delegation techniques are rarely taught, the good news is that delegation is a skill like any other – it can be acquired.

An aspirant or new principal will find it hard to deal with all that needs to be done. And there will be a mental toll. The best advice I can give is to stay in a cycle of:

Set
priorities

Delegate
and review
delegations

Review and
reprioritise

Taking 15 minutes to brief a staff member and then keeping an eye on their progress is a more time efficient option than simply letting them head down a pathway without clarity around what you expect. It will cost you more time in the end if they take the wrong course of action.

I encourage all aspirants and principals to do what you can to feel motivated, productive and energised. Make your own wellbeing a vital part of your daily routine and try to get comfortable with being unapologetic. You are going to cause people to feel uncomfortable and you will challenge them, but don't apologise for that.

The role of principal is great, diverse, interesting and rewarding. Set boundaries; complete one task at a time; make meaningful connections; practice relaxation; and smell the roses. Have a clear idea of what you want to achieve. Work on your resilience.

Chapter notes

1.   Conflict of interest declarations can be interesting. Conflicts of interest occur quite regularly and must be managed well by the board. It could be something as simple as a director recommending a member of their family to human resources (HR) to fill a vacant position, or arranging to direct a contract to a friend's business. Parents on boards immediately have a conflict of interest – determining fees, for example, and annual fee increases. The parent-director derives a financial benefit if the fee increase is kept low.

2.   Subcommittees can vary from school to school. In my schools we had (at the very least): executive (generally recruit new directors and look after principal's remuneration), finance, risk & compliance, and buildings and grounds. If you can influence this, keep the committees to as few as necessary for good governance.

Chapter 3
FORMATION OF YOUR LEADERSHIP SELF

MENTAL TOUGHNESS

My colleagues joke about the Superman metaphor (Drysdale et al, 2014):

> *An individual with the capacity to step in and save the day, he is the opposite of a social movement for change; instead, he is the ultimate rugged individual, standing tall with cape flying, fists on hips, wearing the confident half-smile of a job well done. No problem is very complex for Superman – he arrives out of nowhere, quickly disposes of the fiercest of obstacles, and leaves with the unfailing gratitude of the people. (p 793)*

I know that many principals jest about the metaphor, but when called to think more intently about the role, they endorse it.

I liken the impenetrable steel of Superman to the principal's grit; principals need toughness, not so much to be tough, but to be stoutly resilient and robust.

Mental toughness takes more than cognitive capacity, knowledge about education and understanding of independent schools; it requires a variety of deep-seated character and leadership traits.

Of all the expectations your community will have of you, providing principled and decisive leadership will be forefront; they will want you to lead with a strong hand. To do that, principals need lashings of toughness, either as a natural part of who we are or as something we can work at, learn and adopt.

The literature expounds the various qualities that a principal should have. McEwan (2003), Stronge, Richard & Catano (2008), Sutcliffe (2013) and Watson (2005) all make claims about the traits and qualities of effective school principals. Above all others, I set grit, toughness and character. You will not survive without these qualities.

Grit

Since it was proposed by Duckworth et al in 2007, the concept of grit has been widely discussed. Today it is accepted as a quality required in all CEOs. To me, there is absolutely no question that Duckworth's conception of grit as passion and sustained persistence applied toward long-term achievement is highly appropriate for principal leadership. Grit is the combination of resilience, ambition and self-control that principals need as they pursue long-term goals on behalf of their school. These long-term goals can be referred to as "sustainable goals" – they are geared towards developing outcomes for students that create positive benefits now and into the future. It takes time for the benefits of sustainable goals to take root. They usually involve change and developing new philosophies and new ways of working. Hargreaves & Fink (2006) have written extensively about sustainable leadership, fostering it takes true grit.

I recall a very interesting article by Nick Wolny (2021), a former classically trained musician and a current online marketing strategist for small-business owners, experts and entrepreneurs. Wolny claimed that a growth mindset doesn't improve productivity, but grit does; grit is a better predictor of performance success than talent or mindset.

Grit can be developed proactively at any age. So how do principals cultivate grit in an intentional way?

As Duckworth (2022) notes, you're more likely to persevere through tough times when you're fired up about the end goal. Ask yourself, "Why am I putting myself through this, again?" Paint a clear picture of the final destination for both yourself and others and it'll be easier to get everyone on board. Look for ways to make the long game both inspiring and enjoyable, and you'll have what you need to go the distance.

To me, grit means:

- Being passionate about your mission and persevering for the long haul
- The ability to persist and stick with it when you face obstacles and people who want to find fault in the decisions you make
- Being tough enough to handle the critics and naysayers.

At one of my schools, viability was at risk due to failing enrolments, low community morale and dire financial management. I was given a clear mandate by the board chair to do whatever was needed to float the sinking ship. The chair gave me a long rein to do my work.

I took a pragmatic, no nonsense approach. I was open and honest about what needed to be done. I wasn't soft; for some, I wasn't demonstrating the inherent values of the school, timeless values that dated back to the original philosophical founder from the 1920s.

The number of emails I received from parents who were quite scathing of my approach could have sent me packing. They were demoralising, they hurt, even from people who did not know me. I pushed back – something I hadn't done before as a principal. I called them out. A necessary response that came to feel over-used was, "I find your remarks to be offensive. I will do my best not to take them personally, and work to resolve the issue for the benefit of your child." I had to write too many emails of this type. The emails critical of my decision making contrasted with a parent community that was generally very supportive and appreciative of my leadership. There are various analogies for this phenomenon in schools, where so much of our time is soaked up by an undeserving few. That is when I draw on my grit.

I really had to draw on my grit during strategic planning sessions with boards – no disrespect to said boards intended. As the principal of a school, I was always thinking strategically, plotting a future for the school that was its best evolution, spending countless waking hours (and should-have-been-sleeping hours) thinking about what needed to be done.

Directors don't have the luxury of time, nor is it their job, to dwell on such things. So, those cyclical (every 3–5 years) day-long sessions where the board and executive team came together to think about the school's future required two things from me: a sense of humour and grit. You have to stay the course, keep reminding yourself of the purpose of the strategy session, keep long-term goals in mind. It required me to constantly redirect directors to the purpose and the aim. These are the challenges of a CEO.

Toughness

If grit is the entrée, then toughness is the main course. When I talk about toughness with aspirants, I am referring to the cadre of qualities such as courage, stamina, a strong will, and the ability to transcend seemingly insurmountable odds.

Toughness is a quality of mind characterised by, among other things, a refusal to be intimidated, a determination to complete something you set out to achieve even when things are not going well, and an ability to stay calm and keep your focus when under pressure. It is having a thick skin.

As a principal, I didn't often seek permission. I owned and accepted responsibility. I made it my own way. If I made mistakes and hit a roadblock, I would suck it up, draw breath and soldier on. If there needed to be reparation or restitution, that was ok with me – it was part of the process. I didn't try and control things that couldn't be controlled.

In one of my schools, over a six-month period, I had to defend myself against constant criticism from a director. The director felt that I was not affording sufficient respect to their professional expertise and the contribution that they could make to school operations. At board meetings I was subject to sharp questions that went to the core of the way I led the school and made decisions. Eventually I was required to attend a meeting with the chair, deputy, and director to resolve the "issues." You have to call on all your reserves of toughness when you sit in a meeting with three directors, without any support.

The meeting ended well, but it took some months for me to build the trust and confidence of the aggrieved director. We got there eventually. In this instance I was fortunate that the board chair had good mediation skills. She knew that I was honourable and she wanted a favourable outcome for me and the director.

Reflecting on this trait now, I believe I was mentally tough because I was optimistic. I am generally regarded by colleagues as having an optimistic outlook – not in the "look on the bright side of life" sense, but in having a belief that if you use your common sense and personal resources to plan and take appropriate action, then things will turn out well. Mental toughness also requires you to have an intrinsic trust that people are of good intention. You need to do more than just tell yourself that nothing bad can happen.

When I was the chair of Hunter Region Independent Schools (HRIS), I contacted a man named Mark Bunn to arrange professional development sessions for the principals who were part of the association. Until then, I had little or no concept of eastern wisdom. Bunn introduced us to the tenets that underlie his book, *Ancient Wisdom for Modern Health* (2010). More recently I have come to understand mindfulness, a concept I knew nothing about in my early principal career. The practice of mindfulness is now more commonplace and I understand its benefits much better. I would recommend that aspirants give thought to practices that attend to our consciousness.

These techniques enabled me to train my mind to know that, given past experiences and what I learned from them, there probably isn't anything ahead that I can't deal with.

In addition to abundant optimism, another quality that allowed me to press on was hope. With hope, I could take action and then see results. Without hope, people falter and get derailed from their quest. I had plenty of self-belief, which to me meant having the self-confidence to take on challenges and put in the necessary effort to succeed. My optimistic outlook gave me a positive acknowledgement and expectation about succeeding now and in the future. With hope, I felt I could persevere toward goals in order to succeed.

I've been knocked down a few times in my personal and professional life, as we all have. Each time it was optimism, hope and a positive outlook that gave me the toughness to see things through.

The other quality that ensured I would endure was embracing uncertainty. I didn't need to predict the future. I had to plan the school's future but didn't need to do so with 100 per cent accuracy. Mentally strong people embrace uncertainty, principals in schools need this quality.

Any time a principal is called to take ultimate action on a student's enrolment, to expel them, requires mental toughness. This is such a challenging time for a principal. You have to consider what is best for the school as a whole, what is best for the child, the impact on the parents, and the response from teachers if you don't act. You will likely become acquainted with a human rights commissioner or the anti-discrimination commission, and more than likely a local journalist with an insatiable appetite for drawing attention to wealthy private schools. Anything is possible.

Situations like these are demanding – cognitively, socially and emotionally. They are draining. You need to be able to draw on your toughness and resolve to work through them. Even if your decision is in the best interests of the whole community, it may not meet favour with your board. You may find yourself under intense scrutiny from the aggrieved parent. You will need incredible reserves.

Character

In addition to the general conception of grit and toughness, principals also need character.

What is "character"?

Character can comprise of ethical and moral decision making; honesty, integrity, stamina and drive; the ability to inspire; abundant self-confidence; unflinching passion for the job; sound moral judgement; and social and emotional intelligence.

Ask yourself how you relate to each one of these. Strip out each and write down your reflection (one sentence is enough).

An essential element of the principal's character is the will to take the lead. I have felt I was at my best when I was leading by example. Indeed, unless I led by example, none of the things that I was trying to achieve happened. I always insisted on high standards, which is vitally important in leadership, but I had to walk my talk.

I felt it was my job to set, demonstrate and expect exacting standards of professionalism, modelling core values for staff, students, and the community alike. That was my job, I had to define and set the professional standards that I expected in my schools. No one else could do that. It takes a strong sense of self and who you are as a leader – a strong character – to lead in this way.

Often, coming to a fork in the road when making tough decisions, I felt strong and assured when I could say in a staff meeting, or a parent meeting, "No, that is not ethically or morally right and we won't be doing that. That is not the way we do things around here." But I occasionally found myself in situations where the decision was not mine alone.

At one of my schools, a board director asked me to accept an enrolment from a friend of theirs – a well-known and highly respected member of the community, a community that spanned our school and our major competitor. The potential enrolment would mean three new students, and the family would move from our competitor school. We did not have a place for two of the children, as we had other families on a waiting list.

I had a process of checks in place, and followed this as usual. My business manager checked with the current school of the potential enrolment's family to see that they were not a financial debt risk, they could pay the fees. That was fine in this case. My head of (sub) school would contact the current school to see if there were any behavioural issues that we should be concerned about. It was discovered that the student we had a vacancy for was not a student who would add any value to the cohort and it seemed from the reports we received that they would be terribly disruptive and cause no end of behavioural issues.

I knew I did not want to depart from our procedures and offer this family places for their three children. I went back to the director and told them so, and that I could not proceed with enrolment.

Next, other directors involved themselves, asserting that this family would be an asset to the school, and I needed to make an exception. I reasserted my stance, but to no avail. I was instructed to make the enrolments happen. I followed the instruction. I fought a good fight, but I had to put up the white flag against the collective will of the board.

What did I learn from that? The board are ultimately your employer.

Character, like integrity, is knowing who you are, being true to yourself and acting accordingly. Knowing who you are means holding yourself accountable. If you accept responsibility for all that is required of you as a principal, you must by extension accept that you will be held accountable and take personal responsibility. It's easy to lose your leadership way if you don't have a strong character. Without it, you'll find yourself bending to demands of others and departing from your own values and beliefs.

In each of my roles as principal, I accepted ultimate accountability for the school's performance and success, or lack thereof. Accountability to me meant confronting: behaviour and choices that were inconsistent with school's ideals, values, and beliefs; performance that fell short of all, not just some, of the metrics that matter; decisions on how to spend time and money that were inconsistent with strategic intent. True accountability required me not just to acknowledge and confront behaviour, performance and decisions that fell short, but also to implement real consequences. Consequences can range from direct conversations to course correction to punitive action, but consequences must occur. Without accountability and consequence, words are just words. Your character will be tested when you are held to account.

No matter how lofty, well-intentioned or brilliant your talk is, your character is displayed in your walk (Fiorina, 2021). People in your community may appreciate your talk, but they watch your walk. It is our walk that defines us as principals, not our talk. Actions always speak louder than words.

Authentic charisma is an attribute that must be held by a principal. You are going to be far more effective with it, than without it. I knew I had to be visible, accessible, and available in my schools. I had to have presence; I set the tone and I led through my demeanour and by energetic example. I led effectively through engaging and connected one-on-one and small group interactions, but I also had to command an audience of hundreds. The good news is, you can learn to be charismatic, if it is a trait you want to develop. And you can build grit and toughness too.

Your character should become your beacon, easily observed by your community and the standard by which you will be accountable for your leadership.

In hindsight

I like to think that during my years as principal I maintained a thick skin and a soft heart. All principals and CEOs carry the burden of leadership and must (most of the time) keep cool or maintain composure. It is okay to occasionally show your annoyance in a dignified way, if that is possible. Projecting calm in a storm is essential because during the storm people look to you, as the leader, to rise above the turbulence.

I acknowledge I made a few mistakes, I learned how to forgive myself and move on. You can have a thick skin and maintain a tender heart. It gives you social and political capital. As such a leader, I cared deeply about people but didn't need them to define me. I felt it was important when appointing key staff that I chose people who would complement my leadership style. Sometimes that meant choosing those who were quite different as leaders. This is important – the executive team must have diverse interests, styles, and backgrounds to effectively provide collective and embodied leadership.

With thick skin and a tender heart, I was trustworthy, effective, compassionate and focused.

SELF-LEADERSHIP – YOUR SILVER BULLET

If you want to succeed in this noble profession, to become a principal and sustain excellence in your role, you must place a high value on the quality of your self-leadership. I define self-leadership as your focus on your own self-improvement and professional growth.

It is an often debated cliché that successful leaders aren't born great, but learn through a series of mistakes and lessons and from mentors and opportunities. Effective principals are always learning, and I knew that personal development was the key to continued professional success. I didn't have any hesitation admitting that I wasn't flawless, and I was determined to seek self-improvement. If I did that, I knew my staff would follow suit.

To remain effective as a principal, I had to invest heavily in my ongoing self-development and personal and professional growth. Toward the end of my career as principal, the budget for my own professional development was

$50,000. I was fortunate that my board supported my professional learning without hesitation.

Early career principals and newly appointed principals may not have this kind of budget. It is important that, at the point of signing your contract, you make a strong case for significant professional development. To understand what your PD budget could be, ask colleagues and check in with the CEO of AHISA – they will be able to assist you establish a solid PD budget early on. It is hard to make much progress with your PD budget if you don't start out with a strong foundation.

Importantly, in the absence of a large PD budget, engagement with key professional associations will serve you well in the early years. Key bodies for professional development were discussed earlier in chapter 2.

As mentioned earlier, my leadership journey was a purposeful mix of formal learning, on-the-job experience, learning from colleagues and affiliations, and professional reading. I made commitments to collegial organisations, such as AHISA, the QLD and NSW branches of AHISA, and AIS NSW. These professional bodies provided me with connections, networking opportunities and idea generation. I also committed to associations that added value to the student programs, including sporting associations, and network groups such as the Heads of Independent Co-educational Schools of NSW/ACT (HICES), and the Hunter Region Independent Schools (HRIS).

When successful principals tell me about their leadership journey, it generally follows the same overall mix, with nuanced differences for each principal's context.

I used to love chatting to my colleagues about their sabbatical – I was in awe of those principals who completed the pilgrim walks of Europe, like the Camino Portugués from Lisbon to Santiago de Compostela. There were also highly conscientious ones who would study executive leadership programs at Harvard or Oxford.

To perform at the level of CEO, there is no option but to acquire appropriate business acumen to run your school effectively as businesses/corporation. Anecdotally, principals in independent schools have not warmed to this concept, instead preferring their role to be deemed as educational leader. Much of the current literature endorses this view, claiming instructional leadership as one of the most essential leadership functions for school principals. Because independent school principals lead schools, they do pay attention to pedagogy, teaching and learning, teacher development, instruction, and assessment. However, I always delegated this responsibility to executive leaders in my schools, while never straying too far from the discourse and conversations, to allow myself time to focus on the business side of the school.

Experience is the best teacher. My thesis presented case studies of four principals with between sixteen and twenty-five years experience in independent schools. My research demonstrated that significant factors in the principal being effective in their context included: the experience gained from years of leading independent schools; ongoing commitment to their own growth and development; wisdom gained from reflecting on daily practice; and learning from colleagues and affiliated associations.

You can practice good leadership

Get out of the office!

A leader has courage to see the truth, speak the truth and act on the truth. This means making the tough decisions when required. Don't shy away from this. One successful foray will reap returns and boost confidence. When faced with your first challenge, take your time – seek counsel, prepare and deliver results.

A leader has character to keep going when the going gets tough. The next time you feel rattled, or the troops are messing with your head, take a brisk, 10-minute walk to regroup, then stay the journey. There are plenty of budding political leaders and bush lawyers in your community who will want to derail you – recognise their treachery for what it is.

A leader is humble and empathetic. Your best weapon is communication and collaboration with others. Be prepared to admit what you don't know and where you need help. But at the end of the day, it is up to you to make decisions. Be certain about this. You can consult as widely and deeply as you want, but you must take responsibility. Fess up if you have made a mistake and model how to set it right.

Communicate constantly and consistently, with care and with candour, about where you are, where you are going, and how you are going to get there. Be a problem solver and model this. Show others how to see possibilities, even in the most difficult of circumstances, and empower them to find solutions. They may come naturally to this responsibility, or you may have to coach and train them. This is such a valuable part of being a leader.

In my experience, people always have more potential than they realise – potential to create, overcome, inspire, and problem solve. A leader's highest calling is to tap into that virtually limitless human potential and focus it on the crisis at hand. Strong leadership enables us to get through the bad times so that opportunities can be seized when better times return. Leaders unlock potential in others so that others can do more themselves. In a school context, this contributes to staff feeling valued that they are contributing meaningfully, and to having a higher sense of satisfaction in their work – both of which are good for culture and morale.

As an independent school principal, leading a large and complex organisation, personal and professional life is demanding and unpredictable. I found that when I led myself with distinction, I could excel. Self-leadership sits at the core of effective leadership; however, when a principal has competing demands, and is inevitably time poor, compromises have to been made. It is often the commitment to self that is sacrificed. Avoid this trap.

In hindsight

The stronger my leadership of self the better I could navigate change, the more flexible and responsive I could be and the less reactive or defensive I was. This required a purposeful mix of formal learning, on-the-job experience, learning from colleagues and affiliations, and professional reading. If I attended to myself, I could have greater focus, clarity on where I was headed, and a sense of equanimity and stability. I encourage all aspirants, early career and more emphatically so, career principals to work at being professionally, ethically, physically, intellectually, psychologically and spiritually fit for the job.

The bottom line is, it is all about taking responsibility and ownership – and the buck stops with you!

WORK-LIFE BALANCE – YOU ONLY HAVE ONE LIFE

Creating your optimised work-life balance requires developing an effective daily schedule – which can take a bit of trial and error. Keep working with it and adjusting as needed, and you will soon find yourself with a better handle on time as well as an improved balance in your daily life.

The role of principal is extensive and can be all-consuming – the sheer size of the role can demoralise even the best principals. The job calls you 7 days of every week, there is no let up. You can be up at 5:00am and at it at until 11 o'clock at night. You'd better be passionate about what you are doing because it consumes your life.

Riley et al (2021) report that, according to a national survey. Australian principals are struggling with the highest burnout rates in a decade. According to the latest data, principals and their deputies worked on average at least 55 hours a week, while a quarter of those reported working more than 60 hours a week. It was not uncommon for me to work 70 hours and more each week.

Achieving an effective work-life balance is a derivative of the resilience trait that an effective principal must have. For me, resilience means energy, drive, enthusiasm, perseverance, wellbeing, thick skin, stamina, toughness, and a balanced lifestyle. The best principals get this right. The stressed-out principals and CEOs don't.

The role will dominate your life if you do not learn to manage it. This is a job that can absolutely wear you down and burn you out. If you want to be principal in an independent school in this country – in any school for that matter – the sheer volume of work is a major issue. It is very hard to find quality time in your week to think about the big picture.

You can achieve a reasonable work-life balance as a principal in an independent school, but you must give work-life balance the same purposeful attention you give to all the operational areas of the school.

Parents, teachers, and boards expect the principal to be visible, accessible and available, yet this competes with the principal's sheer workload. It causes significant tension. Most principals suffer criticism from their communities that they are not visible enough. I understand that, but if you were to look at my diary when I worked at MBC, I was on the job at the latest each morning at 7:00am. On average, probably 3 days per week, I could be at work until 9:30pm. Throw in Saturday sport, every Saturday, and other Saturday events that I was expected to attend. If the school has boarders, there will also be Sunday events. The other tension for principals and CEOs is the weight of family expectations. Principals and CEOs must juggle family commitments; it is no longer acceptable to be "married to the job."

Things have changed on that front from when I first started in the role. At that time, there was an unwritten yet well understood standard that the job came first. I felt I had to attend to the job first and foremost, and after the job was done, I could turn my attention to personal and family matters. I have always been a keen golfer, but most golf clubs hold their members' competition on a Saturday. In my first principalship, there was no way I could consider playing – I had to be at school events, mainly sporting events, on a Saturday. The board chair expected it of me – they would be there too, and looking out for my attendance. I found it very hard to resist the expectations of me at the start of my career. More recently, with more wisdom and practice, it has been possible to find time on weekends for self and family. I learned how to manage both.

How to achieve a better work-life balance

You must look at the demands and responsibilities of your personal and professional lives as one.

- Create a realistic boundary between work and after-work hours and stick to this schedule
- Organise your goals and tasks based on importance
- Taking time off from your busy schedule to relax is important for your mental well-being
- Learn how to say no – it becomes very easy to overwork yourself
- Make use of technology.

The most important change I have witnessed over my career is that it is now an accepted norm that a principal is entitled to a family and personal life. Board chairs actively encourage this, as has been the case for me. It means, for example, that you can say to the director of rowing that you can't attend on Sunday because of a family commitment. In my early days. I was expected to shift the family commitment.

The climate for principals now is more supportive of work-life balance. As a new principal you will still likely become overwhelmed with the workload. I would encourage any new or career principal who finds themselves struggling to take the chair of the board and your executive assistant into your confidence – work together on problem solving before things get out of control.

School principals are no different in this regard to many CEOs, general managers, business owners, and the like. Work-life balance is almost a contradiction in terms for everybody these days, with a serious blurring of the boundaries between our personal and professional lives. I say – I have one life. One life in which I need to balance all dimensions. I found that putting in place boundaries between, for example, work, personal and family dimensions didn't work for me. I had 24 hours a day and 7 days a week to manage all my responsibilities.

My approach has always been to have purposeful strategies every day; a well-structured week with a planned program of work, recreation, and rest; and to sustain this right across the year. In the middle of my time as principal, I came to realise that I needed to forget about managing my time and begin managing my energy levels. Colleagues have heard me teach – or, should I say, preach – this as a solution to the all-consuming role.

I introduced new practices into my daily routine that helped me shift from focussing on time to focussing on energy.

I thought long and hard about the people who were draining my energy. I removed the energy vampires (Sharma, 2018) from my personal and professional life. That was an important step.

I worked to reconnect with myself physically, mentally, emotionally and spiritually. That shift had to be made – beforehand, I was all work.

Here are some changes I made: I committed to an hour long walk at 5:00am, instead of working straight out of bed. I ensured that I was out of my office in the mid-afternoon for a long, purposeful walk around the school. I reestablished a good sleep routine. I made sure that I attended to the most challenging aspects of my day's work in the first half of the day. I even experimented with green tea at 3:00pm, and I immediately felt the benefits.

All these things helped energise me, but the thing that still helps most is the diversity of the job. I really love the fact that in any one day I might have a great exchange with my deputy, visit the early learning centre and say good morning to the little ones, and have a chat along the way to the facilities manager – it's the diversity of the role that really energises me.

Attend to yourself

The problem for principals in independent schools is that they commit heavily and invest significant time, effort and energy into the wellbeing of their whole community – they care for their people. It is the principal's job to support all in the community, to guide them, problem solve with them and ultimately protect the welfare of all. Principals provide support for staff as individuals, looking after their personal and professional wellbeing – particularly when the demands of the profession and the challenge of maintaining a work-life balance provoke difficulties.

This takes time and cannot be achieved in normal work hours. Who is looking after the principal? No-one, generally. So, you have to look after yourself. Don't wait for someone else to do it. Your board won't – they may very well do the complete opposite and knock you around. It is up to you – you have been given the responsibility to run an independent school with, on average, 500 students, 90 staff, over 700 parents, and a more than $10M budget – surely you can run your own wellbeing program. If you can't, enlist help – a personal trainer, nutritionist, lifestyle coach. There is plenty of support if you can't manage it yourself.

I met too many principals and CEOs who were fatigued trying to manage the demands of change, decreeing that there wasn't enough time in the day, wishing that things would slow down or somehow get better. "I am too busy," they would cry. I discovered the best method to being match fit was learning to manage my energy to ensure I was highly productive when on-task. This also required attending to time off-task just as diligently.

This daily rhythm is different for different people. It is important to find your peak hours and your troughs, and to purposefully do something, physically or psychologically, to capitalise on or overcome these. I found that this rhythm changed for each stage of my principalship; experience was a good teacher.

I realised that I had much higher energy levels if I started my day with a brisk walk for an hour. I adjusted the timing so that I was able to capture at least 30 minutes of first sunlight. When possible, I inserted a walk in my late afternoon.

Don't underestimate the power of a short, brisk walk during your busy day.

Walking is the simplest and most effective thing I do to manage my work and life. Walking takes little preparation and minimal effort, it requires no special equipment or other people, and it can contract or expand to fit the exact amount of time I have available. When I want to do something that's good for my mind, body and soul, I go for a walk. When I want someone's company, or just want to be alone, you'll find me walking.

Walking in my own company gave me a chance to attend to my mental wellbeing, as well as physical wellbeing.

I have walked along the rivers in Maitland and Brisbane, along the beach where I now live, through national parks, and along Sydney's myriad of stunning tracks. I can feel my stress levels dropping amidst a walk. Exercise increases concentrations of brain chemicals that moderate our response to stress. I felt happier and more elated when I was walking because exercise releases endorphins, which create feelings of happiness and euphoria.

If I ended my day feeling anxious, I knew that a walk would make me feel better. It was always good to go for a walk before a board meeting! I felt noticeably calmer after a walk; I felt relaxed. I know it improved my self-worth and self-image, even though there was no physical change in my appearance; I felt better and felt I looked better.

For many, many years I found that attending church and being involved in school chapel services assisted my spiritual wellbeing. More recently though, I have struggled with the direction that institutional churches have taken. I now attend to my emotional and spiritual wellbeing through the rich experiences of travel. I have travelled extensively through Australia and New Zealand, with untold trips to Africa, Europe, the United Kingdom and Asia.

For me, the benefits of travel included opportunities to learn about and experience new places, cultures and societies. Through these experiences, I gained a deeper knowledge of myself and the world around me. Roaming around Uluru (Australia), Stonehenge and Glastonbury (England), Mont Saint-Michel (France), and the Sanctuary of Fátima (Portugal) has promoted my spirituality and wellbeing.

How to stop thinking about work at 3:00am

One of my biggest challenges has been how to stop thinking about work at 3:00am. I am not alone – this is a modern-day affliction for CEOs and principals across the globe.

Murray (2021) recommends mindfulness to deal with 3:00am waking; and it certainly works for me. There are many mindfulness exercises you can practice, but for me bringing attention to the sound of my breath is the most effective. When I notice my thoughts rising, I focus on my breathing and the sound of my breath. I try to lengthen the inhalation and stretch out the exhalation. I count my breaths, too.

If after 30 minutes or so I am still not asleep, I get up, have a glass of water, open some windows, maybe make a note or two about what is occupying my mind, and then go back to bed. Going to bed with a clear and organised mind, knowing what has to be done tomorrow, is also helpful.

Work stress is inevitable, but it doesn't have to get in the way of a good night's sleep. To avoid thinking about work in the middle of the night, I found a few things help:

- Make a to-do list. The act of writing down uncompleted tasks decreases cognitive arousal, rumination and worry. Making a to-do list for the following day before bed usually helps me to fall asleep faster and stay asleep
- Keep a journal. Writing down my thoughts and feelings, rather than just thinking about them, has helped me to process emotions and reduce stress and anxiety, allowing me a more peaceful night's sleep
- Have regular physical activity. I found that a single instance of moderately intense exercise decreased my restlessness at night

- Practise meditation. I add this because colleagues have told me this really works. Other than the breathwork already mentioned, I haven't made a commitment to make this work for me
- Try a range of "mindless" activities, such as watering the plants; listening to music; spending time with your pet; a walk on the beach; cooking; a long drive, and taking a nap. A nap was the most powerful for me. These activities helped me calm my racing mind, improve my sleep and extend my sleep duration.

If you are having serious sleep problems, don't tolerate it for long. Seek professional help if other techniques aren't making a difference – there are lots of underlying physical and mental conditions that can have an impact on sleep, it's not always "just" stress. A counsellor or therapists can help with techniques to manage stress, too.

The third space

One of the most influential people to have impacted how I manage work-life balance is Adam Fraser. I found Fraser (2012) to be most instructional when it came to prioritising leaving my work at work and showing up at home as a father and husband. Fraser talks about using transitional spaces or "the third space" to reflect, rest and reset – enabling a fresh mindset for each new encounter. This might be between work and home, or between meetings or other tasks.

I learned from Fraser how to transition from work to home more effectively – at the end of the day, my "third space" became Woolworths, where I would shift from principal to husband while getting the ingredients for dinner. From this, I developed a ritual with my wife – each day we would chat on the phone at about 3pm, to debrief our day and plan our dinner and how we would spend the night. Planning our dinner together was fun, and cooking and eating the meal was an evening ritual we would religiously protect.

In hindsight

You and I are so much alike. We only have one life. It is up to me, and you, to choose how we spend every day. There is always a desire to focus on work, but sometimes you just have to put your pen down and focus on self and family. This has been one of my biggest challenges.

You must manage your work, family life and personal life. Manage your energy, not your time, to ensure you are highly productive when on task. Achieving an effective work-life balance is not simply a theoretical concept, it is a function of your personal traits and a derivative of important attributes like resilience. Looking after yourself is a selfish and deeply personal commitment that you have to make, because you will be hard pressed to find anyone else who will.

And never underestimate the power of a short, brisk walk.

Chapter 4
MANAGING KEY STAKEHOLDERS

STAKEHOLDER GROUPS

As a principal you must be judicious in appreciating the context of your school, understanding the needs and aspirations of your community, and knowing the demography of your parent group. From this position you can engage the community to support the school and your goals for it. You only come to know your community through tireless interactions with its members.

Each stakeholder group brings a whole level of voice, expectations, influences and challenges, which the principal has to manage productively for the school's benefit. Fail in this aspect of the role and you perish. Politics is an inescapable part of the life of an independent school principal. I use the term stakeholder in a broad context, meaning anyone who was invested in the welfare and success of my school and our students, including support and operational staff, teachers, students, parents, community members, local businesses that we dealt with, and school board members.

My case study research identified the multitude of community groups and stakeholders that principals in independent schools must manage; they are multi-levelled and complex, as you can see in the table below. I developed this list from reviewing independent schools' websites and school publications, and from transcripts of case study interviews. This list is not exhaustive. To give some context to the depth of community engagement and stakeholder management that is required by independent school principals, my colleague at a school in the west of Ipswich, Queensland, had eight official social media accounts, and a colleague at a large, inner-city Sydney school had ten official parent support groups. As principal, you must meet the challenge of building engagement with key school community stakeholders so that they are willing and able to collaborate with you to support the vision and goals you have for the school.

Internal stakeholders	External stakeholders
The chair and members of the board	The state-based AIS
Teachers, support and operational staff	Teacher unions
Parents, individually and collectively	Universities and colleges
Parent associations and support groups	The wider geographical community
Alumni groups	Local, state and federal governments
Co-curricular clubs	Members of parliament and opposition
Outside hours school care providers	Community services, state protection services and other like agencies
Social media communities	Hierarchy of the affiliated churches
Sponsors, donors and philanthropists	
Ministers of the affiliated local churches	

Consider this list and what it says to you. You will spend an awful lot of your day working with people. Aspirants and principals alike have asked me what they can do to improve their skills in stakeholder management.

I remember back in the early 1990s, as principal of Moreton Bay College, I was trying to get state government approval for the establishment of Moreton Bay Boys College. My good friend Jeff Buchanan (then director of development at MBC) and I had countless meetings with local state members of parliament. This was required because every independent school in our catchment lodged an objection to the new school – they had only one reason, competition. So, Jeff and I had to lobby the politicians. Most of them were completely inert, I must tell you, save for two. The state Minister for Education, Anna Bligh, who would go on to be premier, was one. Minister Bligh was an astute, knowledgeable and savvy political leader. It only took one meeting for her to know the school had to be approved. The other active politician was the local raconteur Con Sciacca, Member of the Federal Parliament for Bowman. Jeff and I nearly fell off our chairs when at one stage, in response to our comment that we were having trouble with the local state politicians, he extorted, "Don't worry about those [word deleted] state members, they have nothing to offer, I will sort it for you."

I'm not sure what happened next, but we got approval very soon after.

The churches were interesting bodies to deal with, each denomination having its own "governance." The governance in churches can be frustrating. All principals in faith-based schools have to deal with church politics, church doctrine and control, and the moral/ethical dilemmas that arise when you are affiliated with a church.

I had a particularly serious issue with my school board at one point, and I was at an impasse. I went to the highest level of governance in the church to share my concerns and plead for intervention to break the impasse. I remember being so well prepared for the meeting at the offices of the most senior administrator of the church. I had my case established, the course of action I sought and the nature of the intervention that I needed. I was hosed down in the first 5 minutes when I heard that the most senior administrator of the Church had no jurisdiction.

I left frustrated and demoralised. It has been said time and time again that churches should not be directly involved in running schools. The Uniting Church in Australia, in Sydney and Melbourne, have moved to dissociate themselves from the governance of schools by having their schools in those cities moved to be separately incorporated.

Principals learn to navigate the church, as they do other stakeholder groups, through experience and by seeking the advice of experienced colleagues who understand the context of church schools. I learned to navigate the church by working hard to understand the organisational culture of the church, how they made decisions, and what important values and beliefs needed to be reflected in the school's work on behalf of the church. I got to know the key personnel and influential members of the church. I worked hard to build connection and key relationships. The church's overarching mission and purpose in developing young adults was important, and I ensured this work was done in my schools.

It was more challenging to deal with the intrusion of the church into the governance and leadership of my schools. I managed this with the support, guidance and advice of the board chair at the time.

The independent sector

There are close to 1100 schools and over 570,000 students in independent schools in Australia. Sixteen per cent of all school enrolments in Australia are in independent schools (Independent Schools Australia, 2021).

The most obvious differences between government and non-government schools come from governance, the role and responsibilities of the principal, and funding. Government schools do not charge tuition fees, non-government schools do.

All government and non-government schools in Australia operate within the constraints of state or territory and federal government legislation, which together impose requirements in relation to financial management, accountability, curriculum, assessment and reporting.

In an independent school, you are on your own. Your school is autonomous and self-managing, there are no central support systems.

I found that the independent school sector was a key stakeholder, a key relationship and significant and positive influence on me as a principal. I always believed that I had a duty and a responsibility to the whole sector because how the public viewed my school reflected positively or otherwise on the whole sector and vice versa.

An article published by *The Guardian* in August 2018 gave a classic illustration of how independent schools are viewed as one, with the headline "Bespoke education": Are Australia's private schools worth the price tag?

As principals of independent schools, we are members of the local state-based association of independent schools, members of Independent Schools

Australia, and many of us are members of AHISA. These memberships require us to represent the sector professionally and to see the sector is held in high repute. I always felt that my school (and my leadership) had to be a strong, effective representative of independent schools.

YOU ARE THE HEAD OF A VILLAGE

Managing relationships and stakeholder influence would weigh heavily on my shoulders as the principal. It would wear on my energy and resources to engage positively and productively with all the groups in each of my schools. Just like a community leader in a small town or village, you are associated with the life of your community: on weekends, attending school events and functions, making social connections. I felt I was viewed by parents as a natural authority – they would seek my advice on topics such as raising their children, how manage screen time and how to reconnect teenagers to family life. I had considerable influence over my families and was even asked to be a mediator in family disputes. In one school, a seventeen-year-old lad left his family home to live with a friend's family. I was brought into that dispute to try and get the lad to return to his home. Eventually he did. I was even asked to oversee funeral ceremonies of members of our community who had died.

As principal, I knew it was my job to keep the community focused, informed and valued. I couldn't afford to impair or fracture relationships with any stakeholder. It required significant skill, judgement, and expertise to manage this, abilities I learned on the job. As a bright eyed and bushy tailed, thirty-seven-year-old principal, I was not aware of how significant community leadership would be.

Being a community leader requires you to value all members of your community, and to be able to connect with all its segments – and many external groups. In all these relationships, you must be able to engender confidence in yourself and your school.

Relationships with parents – caring for their collective wellbeing and helping them develop an affinity with the school – was terribly important to me in my work.

Managing each child's relationships was challenging. It was my role to manage the welfare of all students in my school. On reflection I recognise that children today have far more complex relationships within and outside of school than they did in the early part of my career in the early 2000s. It was quite common for a parent to arrive at the school to collect their child despite clear orders that this was not to happen. I would have to engage the parent and their partner (not the child's biological parent) in the car park and physically intervene. These are the challenges we face when we take on the responsibility of the care of a child.

Schools have always been focused on the needs of the child – their learning, emotional, physical, psychological and spiritual needs. The role of principal has extended to caring for the child's family – their parents, grandparents, extended family or carers. Principals may be called on to enter into family disputes, family court matters and handover arrangements, we may need to meet access and residency requirements, and will certainly encounter other complex situations.

I have had to physically intervene when an estranged parent tried to forcibly remove a child from our school against the child's wishes. I have had teenagers come to my office as a refuge when a parent contacted them by text message saying they would be coming to the school to collect them, against their will. I had to find emergency housing for an eighteen-year-old who was assaulted by their intoxicated father.

There are many demands of the role, but I know that leadership of independent schools is underscored by human leadership. We support and care for the people in our community, build relationships and engage closely with all, while leading with a compassionate heart.

Managing parent relationships

The wellbeing of parents directly affects the school, and parents can also have a lot to learn. At each of my schools, an important role was to help parents understand what it means to have a contemporary, independent school education. For every event our school had, I would try and explain how we did things, and how we did things differently to when they were in school. I had to craft the right messages carefully and strategically. I did a lot of parent education and I valued that part of my role highly; I gradually moved our parents to where I wanted them to be, in support of the school and our goals and plans. I did a lot of writing and speaking, and these were important parts of my role.

There are times when you must be candid, straight to the point and uncompromising. As I write this chapter (in late 2021), all schools in the ACT are gripped by an extended lockdown. I am in the midst of plotting our pathway back to full on-campus learning instead of remote learning. The school's executive team and board had to make a decision about mandating vaccinations; it was a short discussion and easy decision: we would not mandate vaccinations and were comfortable with this.

Having made this decision and having developed a comprehensive risk management plan which I shared with staff, and parents, the ACT government made the decision to mandate vaccinations for school staff. The matter was taken out of our hands.

I had a parent email to say, "I'd be keen to know the proportion of staff that are fully vaccinated now and will be by 1 November. Also, whether my son's teachers are vaccinated."

Sometimes you must offer only a brief explanation and try to avoid defending your decision, as this can result in a cycle of interminable emails. My response was, "I am not prepared to provide you with that information. As a school we are following the Public Health Order and the requirements of ACT Health." The parent accepted my reply and was comfortable with my response.

As a principal there is a real tension between being decisive and firm, and being collaborative. You can resolve this tension if you have a strong, clear and compelling purpose that is visible to your community.

The conversation around COVID-19 vaccinations gave rise to much criticism of and between teachers and parents. The question of whether to be vaccinated or not to be vaccinated caused emotions to run high. I had four staff resign in one of my schools because they refused to be vaccinated; this was common across schools all over the country. Teachers would not meet with parents if parents were not vaccinated. Parents responded with accusations of discrimination. Most states of Australia enforced a public health directive that mandated staff in schools be fully vaccinated, otherwise they could not work with children. Despite the matter being out of our hands, as principals we were still pilloried by some for honouring the direction and (reluctantly for most of us) implementing it.

Principals need a thick skin – here are some excerpts from emails that I received during the implementation of the COVID-19 vaccine mandate:

> *"Well, that was a response that completely lacked courage: in the substantive decision, and the tactically delayed and shallow response."*

> *"Coerced consent is assault. This is no different to rape. Shame on you for participating in that coercion."*

It wasn't all bad, with many parents going out of their way to show support:

> *"Please pass on to any affected teachers – I'm sure you know who they are – my deep appreciation of their courage and sacrifice, and compassion for their situation."*

One of my case-study principals said, "Listening to people, collaborating, is really important. It takes a lot of time, and you will have people disagree with you, but you just go along and deal with that. It is more important that you spend the time collaborating."

This highlights the relationship principals have with parents in a fee-paying structure. You have to invest time in parents; you need parents onside, in your camp. This world, in which principals lead and educate children, is so different from the one most principals grew up in. Such rapid social change makes it more important than ever for schools (and principals) to know the families who come to our schools. Principals need to understand not only what skills and knowledge their students already have and how they learn best, but also how life at home shapes their interactions with school.

To do a good job of knowing my students, I must first discard old assumptions about children and families. Then I must gather information about what life is really like for the children and young adults that our schools teach. The best way to do that is by listening to the people who know our students best – their parents.

It is more important that you engage with your parents, building partnerships and not retreat from them. An aspect of that is to bring parents along with you on the school's journey of growth and change. Parents want and need to know your vision and your plans for the school. Parents are not mind-readers, so unless you make your intentions, goals and aspirations explicit, they cannot support you.

I have been blessed in my career that parents have respected my workday – until emails became the predominant form of communication. Before that, parents' only means of contacting the principal or deputy principal at short notice was by phone – landline earlier in my career and then, of course, mobile.

In my role as head of curriculum at my first school, a parent called me at home around 8pm. My children will tell you, "Don't ring Dad after 6pm" – I can be cranky at the end of a demanding workday. This parent didn't know that. After about 10 minutes it became apparent that the reason for his call, and his wants, could wait until the morning. I suggested that we speak the next day, and quickly came the retort, "I pay your salary." Well, the call ended quickly and that fellow never ventured to call me at home again. It was one of those light bulb moments in leadership: if you stand your ground with firmness, clarity and from a professionally defensible stance, you earn respect instead of the expected chagrin.

In that moment I was establishing another important principle: I would not take phone calls at night from parents unless there was an emergency or crisis.

Independent schools are funded by a combination of parental contribution and federal and state government funding; the majority comes from parents and other private sources. I knew that my parents paid high fees compared to their demographic, and in return for this, parents expected good educational outcomes. If the school, and by extension the principal, fails to meet the expectations of the fee-paying parent, then the parent may choose to withdraw their child and move them to another school. In isolated cases, this may not be a problem. However, if enough disgruntled parents voice their objection in the community and through social media platforms, this can have a negative impact on the reputation of the school and on enrolments.

One thing that has changed dramatically over my time as a principal is the shift in parent expectations around communication. When I first started in the role, I would rarely hear from a parent. If I did, it would be via a formal letter or pre-arranged phone call. Emails were around in the eighties, but it took a decade or two before parents in schools started using emails prolifically and emailing the principal directly. Poorly crafted, hastily written, and careless email responses can damage relationships.

Early on, I established an effective system for dealing with emails. I used Outlook 365 to organise them and my mission throughout each day was to keep my inbox at zero emails.

Zero inbox

Zero inbox was a mindset for me. This is how I managed to keep the emails in my inbox to zero:

- I unsubscribed from emails that I didn't need to read.
- I had a good system of folders, tags, and synchronising with my to-do list. I would shift emails to folders and set a reminder in my diary for any actions that needed to be taken.
- I would only handle an email once. I would respond/ forward, delete, or file for later.
- If I felt an email could be responded to in one minute or less, I would respond. I felt I was better off doing it now than taking time putting it into my to-do list or prioritising it for later.
- I would delegate or forward an email immediately if someone else could deal with it.

I would have emails open all the time and keep an eye on what was popping in my inbox. This strategy goes against the general advice around email management, but it worked for me. I would delete ruthlessly

Also going against general advice, I had email on my smartphone so I could clean up on the go.

In terms of parent emails, I made a commitment to respond the same day with an acknowledgement, and to follow up within 24 hours with a more detailed response. If I needed information from others to respond properly, I would still reply no later than 72 hours after the initial email. I was disciplined about this. I felt that it sent a strong, clear message to parents about my professionalism and how I valued them.

Emails are different to phone calls. I would use emails generally, but when I felt that that there was a communication breakdown, I would pick up the phone. I felt that parents were generally more amicable in a phone call or in a one-on-one meeting. I did use emails to validate decisions that I had made about operational matters.

Another difference between parent expectations in my early career compared to now, is that parents now expect an instant reply. The speed of communication these days can be difficult to manage, but we, as principals, still have to deal with it. It is not uncommon now for a parent to contact the school to advise of a critical incident that has just occurred. Students are quick to fire off a text message to a parent to let them know something has just gone down. As the principal, you can immediately be on the back foot.

A critical incident

In a school setting, a critical incident is an event that causes severe impact, such as significant disruption to the school routine, an emergency management situation, or a threat to the safety of students and staff. It may be sudden or protracted, extremely dangerous, involve police or emergency services personnel, and generally be outside the normal range of experience or expectation of people affected. These events do happen in schools and they test the leadership skills of principals.

Around the middle of the day in June 2007, with students still in classes but soon to go to lunch, we had a torrential downpour. It seemed like the storm cell was right on top of the school. The storm caused widespread flooding in Maitland.

From my second-floor office window, I watched the black clouds swirling around and the rain bucketing down. I knew we were in trouble and that if children were out in the storm they could be injured. I went straight into the grounds, keeping out of the downpour by sheltering under the verandah of the library. I watched raging water rushing through the campus in violent torrents.

It was from the verandah of the library that I managed the critical incident. I called for a lockdown. The alarm sounded telling all students they were required to stay in classrooms, or if they were outside a room, to move into the nearest. Students in a lockdown are to hide and stay as silent as possible. It took around 45 minutes for the worst of the storm to abate and the torrents of water to subside. I ordered all students and staff to remain indoors for their lunch and not to move around the campus. The dreadful weather continued into the afternoon and overnight.

Social media has become the bane of principals' existence over the past two decades. Sites like Myspace and LinkedIn gained prominence in the early 2000s but didn't cause any great disruption.

Sites like Flickr caused problems for schools and wellbeing teams as students took up the opportunities they offered with some vigour, but they didn't cause principals any personal/professional challenges.

YouTube was launched in 2005, creating an entirely new way for people to communicate and share with each other across great distances. However, it didn't disrupt my workflow too much.

Facebook was launched in 2004 and first crossed my radar in 2006. All sorts of Facebook groups began popping up, which could easily publish views about the school and the principal's leadership without any accountability. And so principals became easy targets. The Rate my Teacher website was launched in 2001 and went rogue as it was widely used to degrade principals and teachers.

Social media opportunities

While the drawbacks and hazards of student social media use are well documented and understood, social media offered many opportunities for schools, including:

- A communication and collaboration platform for students
- A space for online learning and networking
- A tool for engagement
- A vehicle for creative demonstration
- A tool to enable students to experience their global community
- A research tool and way to connect with experts
- A way to help students gain wider knowledge
- A pathway for students to be able to access quality information beyond what the teacher can provide
- A way to help students become independent learners
- A channel for obtaining daily news.

Social media has become a great online learning platform for students. It offers so many opportunities to share knowledge and experience in a fun and exciting way.

Today, there is a tremendous variety of social networking sites, and many of them can be linked to allow cross-posting. This creates an environment where users can reach the maximum number of people without sacrificing the intimacy of person-to-person communication.

I mention social media and communications because they directly impact your work on building positive, beneficial relationships with your community. Navigating these waters requires its own communication acumen.

I recall a Facebook page set up not so long after I started a new position, back in the late 2000s. I had commenced a performance review process on a long-serving senior leader at the school, which ended abruptly when the senior leader literally walked out. They then commenced a campaign of misinformation to undermine trust and confidence in my leadership.

I had also expelled fifteen year 9 students. So, the knives were out. The Facebook page was designed to have me removed as principal. It was called *Say goodbye to Paul Teys*. I survived the targeted Facebook campaign to remove me, but it took some toughness and at times aloofness.

Without the confidence of the community, embodied through quality relationships and eager engagement, it was hard for me to establish a footing from which I could effectively lead my schools. This confidence doesn't happen by chance or by the authority of the position; it happens due to the conscientious effort to nurture ethical relationships every day, in every interaction. Each school is its own community, with a unique context, and the goals, aspirations, and capabilities of its students, teachers and surrounding community reflect its purpose.

Loss of a community member

School principals experience death and tragedy all too often. A friend and colleague of mine had to deal with eighteen deaths in his inner-city Sydney school community in his eighteen years as a principal. He was called upon to be a counsellor, pastor and minister. He had to draw on all his traits of compassion and empathy, from visiting the grieving families in their homes to assisting families at a very practical level – arranging funeral services and even giving the eulogy. There were times when a death involved a coronial inquest or a Workcover investigation. Highly honed media and communication skills are required at times like that. These skills can be developed with appropriate training from companies that work in this space – they are easy to find.

I found that one way to develop my capabilities in this space was to examine case studies in the media. Sadly, there will be examples you can learn from.

What also worked for me was establishing a partnership with a marketing/communications company that could support me in presenting the school's image to the community. In cases of crisis, where the school might become a matter of interest to the wider community, it is great to have a media expert in your corner.

Many principals have supported families when a parent dies. For children and young people, and parents, losing a family member without notice or preparation is a terrible event. Suicide is particularly confronting and challenging.

I have had to lead my school(s) through the emotional and practical challenges arising from the passing of students, staff and parents on several occasions. While not all leaders will face tragedies, you are likely to find yourself confronted by these experiences at least once during your tenure. Death requires school leaders to act with compassion and care. They must maintain an awareness that they're modelling for young people how to grieve – even while grieving themself. Few better examples of servant leadership exist. Servant leadership is a philosophy and practice of leadership where leaders want to serve rather than lead, with the desire to help others (Greenleaf, 1970).

You may have heard of the superstition that bad luck comes in threes. For me, 2020 was a year that bore that out.

We had three major events that really rocked the school. First came fires in the Hunter Valley, which closed more than 200 schools; then came a freak storm, which hit our school like a cyclone, causing us to close for a day while staff worked to clean up; and then, of course, came COVID-19.

While one might assume that a principal acts naturally in these moments of crisis, as if by some intrinsic grace, that is unlikely. Instead, principals must act intentionally and in a well-planned manner. Whether confronting natural disasters, a pandemic, or an individual's death, very intentional leadership is required.

The communication skills required to manage tragic circumstances are the same as those that principals need when managing critical incidents. I felt that principals, myself included, were on steep learning curves when it came to managing the waves of COVID-19. But you don't need to learn these skills in the heat of the moment. Aspiring and new career principals can hone their communications skills with stakeholder groups in a variety of ways:

- Engage a media and communications consultant. Such supports are now more common, more readily available and more competent than in the first half of my principalship career
- If you employ a communications manager in your school, use them to support your communications. Elicit their expertise when, for example, you have to write a response to a challenging parent email. I had a tremendous communications manager at one of my schools and her work was incredibly valuable

- Adopt rules and strategies around your emails, key principles that you don't compromise on. One errant email can do immeasurable damage
- Engage a coach – someone who is at the end of a phone call or email to review critical emails, phone calls and meetings.

Key principles for emails

If you accept that emails sent from your school email account are for business purposes and that any email sent, received, created or stored may be viewed, you can keep yourself from getting into difficulty with emails. Some email rules:

- Emails should be professional and respectful in tone
- Use a clear, instructional subject line
- Keep emails succinct and precise
- Include a signature with your phone number and professional social media links
- Add the email recipient's address after composing the email to avoid sending an unfinished/unedited message
- Check the recipients' addresses before sending
- Spell check should be enabled, and grammar checked before sending emails
- Use CC judiciously
- To respect others' time and inbox capacity, limit replies to those who need to know the information being conveyed
- It is best practice not to forward without permission, or at least to review all content that will be forwarded to avoid sending sensitive information
- Avoid using ALL CAPS in email communications – this reads like you are shouting
- Manage your turnaround/response times – I had a rule to respond to emails both internally and externally within 24 hours.

I knew that all the forms of communications that I used with members of my school community and the wider community, used effectively, would assist me to develop great, long-term relationships with our "customers." I knew that satisfied customers would recommend our school to a colleague or friend with school-aged children, leading to new business. Positive, enduring relationships were good for the school's success.

Financial sustainability

Private funding contributions through the payment of fees increase the school's accountability to parents. The reality for independent school principals is that they need to ensure their school remains competitive to survive, consistently meeting high parental expectations for the development of students academically, physically, spiritually, emotionally and socially.

Independent schools require parents to pay school fees, which represent a significant proportion of the total operating income required to run their schools. The operating income not only covers the education of students, but also pays for the costs of managing a large, not-for-profit business. This was the situation for the four case study principals in my thesis.

One of these principals, during the case study interviews, said, "We rely on parents' fees to keep our schools afloat – it does come with expectations from parents, to deliver on our promises and all we say that our schools will do." A lesson for the new principal: keep your communications team in check – under promise and over deliver.

There is a lot at stake in independent schools if principals are not effective at sustaining the school's enrolment market share. At risk are the reputation of the school in the community, the financial viability of the school, and long-term sustainability if enrolments decline. The high stakes are due to the tension that arises between the competitive enrolment market and the high fees that the schools charge. Like any corporation, the principal as CEO must see that their school, as a business, is solvent and that their financial future is secure. This means managing parents' needs and expectations.

There are cases of independent schools moving from single sex to co-educational due to falling market share. Other independent schools have amalgamated to boost market share. One school in regional NSW made the decision to go co-educational, with the principal at the time saying, "The decision will ensure the growth of the school into the future."

Mackay saw the merger of two long-established independent schools. Each single-sex school was struggling to attract enrolments against the other competition in the area, especially following the recent establishment of a new independent co-educational school. The respective boards felt the merger would ensure their viability.

And in Melbourne in the 2010s, Kilvington Girls Grammar turned co-educational. The board decided to convert because, with a roll of 500 students and about fifty girls at VCE level, the school wasn't big enough to offer the breadth of subjects required. They were struggling to be viable as a small, single-sex girls' school.

The point is that independent schools are vulnerable to market forces – their sustainability is not to be taken for granted. While the risk to schools is low, it is nonetheless a matter of concern for the local school board at any independent school. And consequently, a matter of significant stress and accountability for the principal.

By virtue of my contract of employment, I was expected to ensure that my schools met the standards of social and financial accountability applying to all corporate entities or charities in Australia. Under the Australian Charities and Not-for-profits Commission Act 2012, entities that are registered charities and not-for-profits have obligations. These include keeping financial records and operational records, reporting their information annually and complying with ACNC governance standards.

Ten strategies to build and sustain quality relationships

1. Talk to others about what they want to hear. People often hear only what they want or need. The things our school communities want to hear most is how, as principals, we can serve their goals, interests, ideas, experiences and aspirations. Talk about that, and you'll get and hold people's attention without difficulty.

2. Invest in learning how to communicate more effectively. This will pay off in every aspect of your professional and your personal life. The best

principals are all master communicators who have learned how to take control of even the most challenging situations, who understand the art of persuasion, and who know how to recognise and use persuasive strategies.

3. Be grateful. Make it a habit to thank others for everything they do to support you. A simple thank you makes others feel appreciated. You benefit in return by having good feelings about making others feel good. And you also benefit by making others think better of you, making them want to do more good things for you in return.

4. Give genuine, sincere compliments. When you compliment someone about a trait, skill, accomplishment or possession, it gives them feelings of recognition and value. The more you pay close attention to your staff and individuals in your community, the more important they feel. When you pay compliments often, even on small things, it helps build rapport. But don't overdo it; ensure it is authentic and comes from a natural place in your values and beliefs. Public recognition is important, such as at a staff meeting if appropriate.

5. Act honourably and treat others with respect. Always do the right thing, even when no one's watching. That's how you build a positive personal brand and reputation. Reputation isn't purchased; it's earned. Nobody cares how much you know until they know how much you care. This is so apt in schools where principals' work is all about people and relationships. I used this to govern my attitudes, thoughts, words and actions. I liked to show people I cared, that was my foundation.

6. Identify personal core values and ethics. Clarifying your core values and ethics highlights what you stand for. Your core values also represent your uniqueness and personal style. They guide your behaviour and provide you with a personal code of conduct. When you honour your core values consistently, you experience fulfillment in every part of life. And when you don't, you become incongruent in your business practices.

7. Success comes easily when you always act with honesty and integrity. Good ethics require dealing honestly in your business, backing up your products and services, and treating everyone fairly. A lack of business ethics endangers your future success and jeopardises your reputation. Always practice good ethics.

8. Remain true to your authentic self. Remaining true to your beliefs helps you sincerely connect to others. Pretending to be something you're not makes doing business hard. You can't manipulate your personality to gain approval or avoid disapproval. You can continually reflect and evaluate yourself as a person. Authenticity isn't defined by your title, position or role. It's all about being true to your heart and your choices. This requires you to trust yourself, embrace your uniqueness, share your gifts, and learn to be present in the moment.

9. Take responsibility for your success; cultivate confidence independent of all external factors, especially the things beyond your control. Confident people talk assertively, strike an assured pose and use a certain tone of voice. Confidence allows you to be tough in business, but tough doesn't mean you can't still be friendly and approachable. Having true confidence is about always being daringly honest and truthful.

10. Tackle problems with a positive mental attitude. The flow-on effect of positive thinking is that you develop the capacity to solve problems through constructive action. A positive mental attitude, an optimistic approach, lets you build strengths and overcome weaknesses. It helps you realise you're born for greatness because within you is the power to make any dream a reality.

THE IMPORTANCE OF PRODUCING HIGH-QUALITY GRADUATES

At the core of my work as principal was a heartfelt dedication to student outcomes. That is the reason I became a teacher in the first place. I loved teaching. I really wanted to shape young people's lives, inspire them and educate them. I wanted to show them they could be something more wonderful than they ever thought possible. The impact a teacher has on a young adult continues into the next generation. It makes sense that one of my core values as a principal was to ensure that each student graduated from my schools with hope and the anticipation of a bright future.

As a principal, I learned that it is the quality of graduate that sells our schools and I always strived to ensure I had strong, sustainable enrolments to support the school's viability. I believe that the school's reputation rested with my focus on ensuring we had high quality graduates who could represent us admirably.

I made a deep commitment to making a difference in the lives of our students and our community. I was always concerned for holistic student outcomes, educating the whole person based on high expectations for all students. I maintained uncompromising high expectations of all teachers that set and supported excellent student outcomes.

I was able to resolve the tension that existed between a focus on academic outcomes and a focus on holistic outcomes by working hard to ensure both outcomes were given priority. I knew that my schools, being independent schools in a market-driven, competitive environment, would be judged by the academic results of our students and the quality of the graduates. The expectation and anticipation that this created in the school community manifested itself as real and subliminal pressure on me to perform. Whether right or wrong, the principal's performance in many independent schools in Australia is judged by the annual release of the Australian Tertiary Admission Rank (ATAR).

The release of ATAR scores and year 12 certificates (in each state) triggers the marketing and communications teams showcasing the high achieving students. This causes a dilemma for principals. Principals in independent schools are genuinely committed to holistic outcomes – academic outcomes and personal qualities – yet the community's sensational interest in the highest achievers means that the annual release of league tables seized the focus, at least for the months of December and January. The expectation from parents that our school would figure in the top 100 schools (in NSW) was enormous, in fact intense.

Alumni – past students' associations

Given the age of most independent schools, many have significant numbers of past students. Some schools in Australia are older than 150 years.

When a student graduates from one of these schools, they become part of an extensive past students' network, which are typically respected communities.

This layer of the independent school context creates challenges and opportunities for principals in large, independent schools. To be effective in their roles, principals have to engage with these communities strategically and intentionally.

Being part of the past students' associations presents alumni with the opportunity to access an extensive network of fellow past students from around the world. The schools work hard to ensure that former students remain connected, and principals know it is their job to have in place staff and programs to strengthen bonds between the school and its past students.

Prime ministers Edward Barton and Malcolm Turnbull (Sydney Grammar), Alfred Deakin Stanley Bruce and Malcolm Fraser (Melbourne Grammar), Robert Menzies (Wesley College), John Gorton (Geelong Grammar and Shore), Gough Whitlam (Canberra Grammar) and Tony Abbott (Riverview) all attended independent schools in Australia.

This highlights the fact that parents have very high expectations of independent schools – they buy an education expecting an outcome based on the school's alumni.

One of the main benefits to having a strong and successful past-students network is philanthropy. Principals and their key support staff work hard at securing charitable acts and other good works – like volunteering of time or efforts that help students and the school more generally. Some alumni donate money, often large sums, to support or create capital development, such as new buildings or scholarship funds. For others, acts of philanthropy can mean an annual donation to the school's art show or concert, or supporting overseas tours by providing clothing and equipment.

Philanthropic income is a key item in the yearly budget, especially capital budget, in independent schools where there is vibrant and successful philanthropic activity. A colleague of mine at a very old independent school in Hobart is one of the country's best in advancement work, setting himself annual goals and targets, and prepared to be held accountable for fundraising targets as part of his annual performance.

The philanthropic actions of past students – the legacies they have left – are key to developing teaching and learning facilities, as well as providing funds for future projects that enable our schools to continue delivering outstanding education.

Dame Quentin Bryce, who served as the 25th Governor-General of Australia from 2008 to 2014, was an old girl of Moreton Bay College (MBC). It was a significant honour for me as principal to get to know her. It was also my responsibility to ensure that MBC would produce more graduates of such distinguished standing.

When I was at Fairholme College in Toowoomba during the 1980s, I had the incredible fortune and privilege to coach Cathy Freeman OAM. I can recall vividly how Cathy wanted to run 100m and 200m, not the 400m, but my colleague Anne Brownlie and I felt that she was better suited to the 400m. You could imagine my joy when Cathy went on to become the Olympic champion for the women's 400m at the 2000 Summer Olympics in Sydney, at which she lit the Olympic cauldron. Cathy was an inspiration to her fellow students at Fairholme and much loved in the boarding house. To watch her run was a joy. Cathy was awarded Australian of the Year in 1998 and the Order of Australia Medal in 2001.

I recall when I was a young teacher working in Toowoomba, Queensland, I had an armchair ride watching one of the most spectacular rivalries in Australian sport unfold: Jason Little and Toowoomba Grammar v Tim Horan and Downlands College. Both were two of the best centres Australian Rugby has produced. I didn't teach either, but in a country town like Toowoomba it was hard not to be part of the fun. While he was at school, Jason and I played club cricket together with side, Metropolitans, where I was captain. Jason was an outstanding cricketer and I felt if he committed to cricket like he did to Rugby, he could have played for Australia. The rugby matches between the two schools were fantastic, and Jason and Tim went on to forge a breathtaking centre partnership for Australian Rugby between 1989 and 2000.

Many parents in independent schools where there is incredible success at sport do expect special programs, opportunities and development for their child. They sit on the sidelines of the rugby and netball matches played all over the country on a Saturday morning, hoping and praying that their child might represent Australia.

I had to work hard to ensure that the past students remain connected to the school; it was my job to have in place staff and programs to strengthen those bonds.

Past students often give artefacts and heritage memorabilia to the school's archives. Scholarships provided by past students provide the opportunity of an education in our schools when a family's own financial situation would not allow it.

Many schools offer scholarships to Indigenous students. Barker College, for example, has three campuses that provide Indigenous education, Darkinjung, Ngarralingayil and Dhupuma, recognising the importance of upholding Aboriginal and Torres Strait Islander cultural identities as Barker strives to close the gap educationally. Many independent schools in Australia provide similar programs.

A colleague in a large, Sydney boys' boarding school had a goal to grow their endowment so that they could continually provide the opportunity for a secondary education at his school to 100 potentially outstanding students from families with proven socio-economic need. With these scholarships, many more children can now access education at a school where the annual fees could be more than $30,000.

These programs are part of the schools' social justice policies. It a natural part of the principal's role – and boards and governments expect it – to provide for disadvantaged children and youth. In addition to scholarship funding and fee-paying programs, students can access the businesses and companies that are run by past students. This opens opportunities for apprenticeships and traineeships, internships, university graduate programs, and casual and part-time employment, as well as mentoring and coaching. The past students' association is a huge asset for the students.

Managing and fostering student networks requires expertise and astuteness, relationship-building and negotiating skills. You can develop these in your current role by helping out the alumni manager (or equivalent) at your school – take the opportunity to engage with past-students and make meaningful connections. Attend alumni events and offer to make introductions to past students you know and have a good relationship with.

It is the principal's job to nurture and manage the past students' association and build productive relationships with alumni. The principal requires political acumen to manage this part of the independent school context.

Building an image of a graduate's future

As a principal I purposefully raised parent expectations that their child would graduate with personal qualities that would enable them to go on to be successful. Students could expect meaningful opportunities after they graduated, to take on leadership roles, and to be productive contributors to society.

This meant I had to ensure that the outcomes matched the claims I had made. The claims must be more than rhetoric. In high fee-paying schools, maintaining prestige is unashamedly about excellent graduate options after year 12, which includes entry to university. It is not an unreasonable expectation from parents given that the public relations and marketing of our schools certainly imply this is the case.

On their websites, independent schools list the academic results, the university destinations, the significant accomplishments, and employment destinations of alumni. Schools share the success stories in the hope of convincing parents that, in addition to buying an education, they are buying a future of optimism and promise.

Independent schools purposefully raise parental expectations that their graduates can go on to be society's leaders. I think all principals are the same – we want our alumni to serve as a shining example of the kind of people that our schools produce. The school community expects the graduates of our schools to go on to be leaders, to be highly successful in life. The claims made in the school's public relations and marketing are purposefully made by the principals in these schools.

I picked up the following statements from the websites of some large, independent schools in Sydney:

> "Results were nothing short of outstanding."

> "The only school in the state with students achieving more first places was [our] school."

> "I am confident they will have much to offer in the years to come."

Principals know that their leadership and their school's programs and opportunities are designed to produce the outcomes for graduates that the community expect. The school's key messages about graduate destinations and their success after year 12 add to the parents' expectations, which results in demands on the principal to produce. Principals are under significant pressure to ensure that parents' expectations are being met and that the school caters for each individual child.

This is a dilemma for principals of independent schools. The publishing of league tables at the end of the academic year by the *The Sydney Morning Herald*, and merit lists by NSW Educations Standards Authority (NESA), means that principals have to keep their eye on academic results. How important is it that a school receives publicity based upon the top 1 per cent of students, or the top 10 per cent, or the ATAR mean? It mattered most to me that each and every graduate had quality options after year 12. Governments should ban the publishing of year 12 results.

I felt I was building an image of a student's future as a means of providing a competitive edge. Parents pay fees and because of this, they had high expectations of our school to deliver excellent outcomes for their child. Because principals are aware of their responsibility to meet parents' expectations, they commit fully to ensuring that students graduate with opportunities, and a bright future.

But principals must strike the right balance between the pressure they face, parental expectations and the impact of these on the kids stuck in the middle. A survey of year 12 students (North, Gross & Smith, 2015) confirmed that HSC exams (in NSW) are a source of major stress on adolescents. The research, from schools across Sydney, showed that 42% of year 12 students registered anxiety symptoms high enough to be of clinical concern. The study – by the University of NSW School of Education – showed what principals have known for a long time, year 12 can be highly stressful for students. While this research looked at the NSW context, it is not peculiar to NSW – the pressure to perform is felt by all Australian year 12 students.

Major school assessments like the HSC are high stakes, where the results of exams have major consequences for the student. In Australia, student performance in year 12 determines university entry, which means marks might determine career paths and earning potential.

Students in the research claimed that they became more result-focused, prioritising the outcome of tests over the process of learning, or simply feared failure. It is a grim situation that principals and their schools must manage.

Holistic student outcomes

During the case study visits that informed my thesis, all four principals I interviewed spoke of their compelling purpose. In each case, that was an unwavering focus on all students and their learning needs. When I unpacked this, they were talking about more than academic learning – they know they are responsible to students as young people who are in the process of learning how to be good citizens. They know their work is to ensure students graduate with quality academic outcomes *and* as young people of good civic and social character. As one principal put it, "It's learning who you are, what your role is going to be and are you going to be a good father, a good husband, partner, a good local citizen."

Holistic education is a philosophy of educating the whole person, beyond core academics, as a means of improving student outcomes. It is a belief that students need more than just a strong foundation in a core curriculum – they also need to be supported by a community and to develop a compassionate understanding of the world around them.

Principals set the tone for whether learning environments will focus on academic-centric or holistic learning concepts, or anything else for that matter – it could be the emphatic development of faith. In a nutshell, holistic education is a comprehensive approach where schools seek to address the emotional, social, psychological, physical, ethical and academic needs of students.

How do principals do this? I emphasised creating and sustaining a positive school environment and providing students with whole-child supports – services that support academic and non-academic needs. Principals leading schools, on behalf of their communities, teach children and young adults to reflect on their actions and how they impact the local and global community, as well as how to learn from the community around them.

Principals attend to the holistic outcomes by purposefully designed leadership and service activities. And leadership isn't just for the year 12 cohort, leadership opportunities are provided across year levels and across a myriad of activities. Case-study principals in my research spoke with pride of the opportunities that are provided to students in their schools.

Many schools have extensive co-curricular programs that give students opportunities to excel beyond the classroom. Sport, drama and music feature prominently in the co-curricular activities available at independent schools, but the list of options and combinations for students to choose from is extensive. It is common for schools to have extensive sporting and creative and performing arts opportunities, including media production; clubs and committees such as student representative councils and social justice groups; chess programs and competitions; debating, mooting and public speaking; and outdoor education programs.

Many independent schools have outdoor education campuses on large landholdings in stunning remote and regional locations that host camps and excursions, and sometimes provide long-term residential accommodation.

I developed strategic goals that enabled me to make decisions about which educational programs I would offer. Some programs developed included courses, leadership and community service programs, co-curricular programs, extensive outdoor education programs, equestrian and cattle teams, exchanges and overseas tours, supporting and sponsoring schools in underdeveloped countries, and Indigenous scholarships programs.

One of the flagship service programs at Hunter Valley Grammar School was to support Jabulani Primary School, near the Victoria Falls airport in Zimbabwe. Some students at Jabulani Primary, even those as young as five years old, had to walk 8 kilometres to and from school every day. As I would have emergency drills in my schools, the children who attended Jabulani learned and practiced what to do if a lion or elephant crossed their paths. Many students might only get one meal a day. We helped the school community build a sustainable vegetable and fruit garden, which the children maintain alongside their teachers, and which provides additional sustenance. We also helped build and stock a school library, giving the students access quality reading materials.

I developed the partnership with the Jabulani School as one of my strategic priorities to ensure that the young adults who graduated from my schools were people of calibre, able to be fine citizens in the communities where they would live, work and lead. One of the case-study principals said:

"My job is to provide a rich, holistic experience for my students ... so they get some idea about what it is to be human, and what it is to be a creative human, and how magical that can be, through drama, sport and music. [They learn] to be intellectually and emotionally fit, and to be aesthetically aware."

I unashamedly created high parental expectations by claiming that our school's graduates would get excellent results to enable them to access their desired courses at their preferred university. It wasn't hollow or reckless to do so, I put all my personal effort and leadership acumen into ensuring this was the case.

There was a risk associated with this, at least in my experience. If a student did not get, for example, the HSC results or ATAR that they or their parents wanted or expected, they would hold me accountable.

To manage this, I had to make sure that the expectations I was raising were contextual and realistic. To do this, you need to know your students, their capabilities and aspirations really well. You need to do astute futures planning with them, so they come to the end of year 12 with authentic options that they are pleased with. That usually means a key division/unit in the school dedicated to year 12 destinations.

In hindsight

It is terribly important that you know and understand your independent school's context, which is local and positioned in the wider independent school context in Australia.

This context requires an acute understanding of what it means to be not-for-profit. I can't understate the importance of a business model that generates surpluses so you can, as principal, reinvest in the school for its growth, competitiveness and to serve the needs of fee-paying parents who, in the case of a preschool to year 12 enrolment, could be making a fifteen-year investment in your school. Fee paying parents rightfully have expectations, and they can have hard-nosed expectations drawn from a commercial perspective too. I have found parents treat paying school fees like a business transaction, similar to the transactions they have with their solicitor or accountant. They pay you to deliver an outcome.

Building and maintaining relationships is at the heart of being an effective principal. If you can't connect with others, you can't do your job – which is to lead people. However, it can sometimes be hard for a new principal to form relationships with stakeholders in the school. My experience tells me that you should do everything you can to get to know your community on a personal and professional level; understand what motivates and drives people, and what they value. Try not to always focus solely on work and instead invest in developing professional camaraderie. It is important that you don't succumb to the bear trap of isolating yourself in the job or distancing yourself from your community. Take every opportunity to engage. Make it part of your daily ritual to engage with as many in your community as possible.

Chapter 5

PRINCIPAL AS CEO

RESEARCH FINDINGS

The most significant finding from my thesis was that principals in independent schools in Australia are chief executive officers (CEOs). My own experience bears this to be absolutely true. There is no equivocation on my part, or that of the four case-study principals involved in my research.

Being a principal in an independent school in Australia is a complex and demanding role. It is multi-faceted and carries responsibilities akin to that of the CEO of a medium-sized, not-for-profit company or corporation in Australia. There are no shareholders in not for-profit companies, but in these school-businesses, there is a multitude of stakeholders.

An independent school principal is expected to effectively discharge all the responsibilities of a CEO, be answerable to the school board and carry overall accountability for the organisation's operations and outcomes. Principals are required to enact their role according to a typical representation found in the literature, that of educational leader, and as a CEO of a not-for-profit company. It is the nexus of these two conceptions that makes the role unique in this country. Blackwood (2019) claims that "the role of principal of an independent school in Australia is often compared to that of CEO of an ASX200 company."

Independent schools in Australia are businesses, run like any business or corporation; they must be financially viable and deliver services and benefits that the customer (parents and students) wants; otherwise, their viability is at risk.

YOU ARE THE CEO

A CEO can be defined as the highest-ranking individual in a company or organisation. As a principal, I was the most senior executive, responsible for the overall success of my school as a business. The buck stopped with me. I had proper input from the board and my executive leaders on major decisions, but I was the ultimate decision-making authority.

I have observed throughout my time as a principal that many of my colleagues were reluctant to be compared to a CEO, preferring to be viewed as the educational leader, pedagogical leader, instructional leader, and a rash of other adjectival leaderships that relate to teaching and learning. Well, that is a big part of the role, but independent schools in Australia are businesses, run like any business or corporation – they must be financially viable and deliver services and outcomes that teachers, parents, and students want.

For principals in independent schools, there is a tension between being the chief education officer and the chief executive officer. Many do not like having to be the chief executive officer, running the school as a business with key financial performance indicators that must be met. Others are more comfortable with that. If we consider this as a spectrum, know that you will occupy all points on the spectrum at some stage.

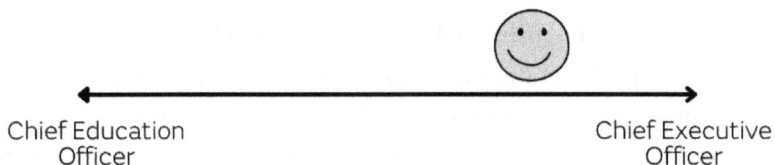

Chief Education Officer   Chief Executive Officer

When I was the principal at Moreton Bay College (an all-girls school) I was provoked and challenged by parents of the school with sons to establish a boy's school. So, I set about establishing Moreton Bay Boys College. MBBC today has more than 500 boys, conveniently located 2km from the girls' school. This is an example of a principal behaving in the same vein as a CEO from the corporate world.

Under company law, businesses cannot operate unless they are solvent, which means the business is able to pay its debts when they fall due for payment. Schools are no different, and I was judged the same way. The school has to generate enough revenue through government funding and fees paid by parents to meet the operational expenses: salaries; interest on borrowings; tuition related expenses; utilities and insurances; administration costs; technology and infrastructure; capital expenses and asset development.

Like a CEO, the principal is the head of the executive team and manages the day-to-day operations of the school, its people and resources. The principal, like the CEO, implements the strategy approved by the board and ensures that the organisation's structurge and processes meet the strategic and cultural needs of the organisation (AHISA, 2011).

Many parallels between the CEO in the corporate world and that of the independent school principal can be drawn.

Degenhardt (2015, p 8) reflected:

> *Leaders of independent schools can learn much from the corporate sector [and many independent school boards include individuals with corporate backgrounds and experience]. A more corporate approach emphasises strategic direction ... It changes the focus from inputs (lessons taught, staff employed, students enrolled, funding secured) to outputs (effective learning, achievement of the school's mission, satisfied stakeholders). It holds people more accountable for their actions, and their performance ... using the best from the corporate sector can, however, assist schools to become 'great' at what they do.*

From my experience, this is a non-exhaustive list of what the principal/CEO of an independent school in Australia is responsible for:

- Governance and board relations
- Strategic/visionary leadership
- Education leadership
- Student engagement and wellbeing
- Staff leadership, development and wellbeing
- Clubs, activities and societies
- Parent support groups and affiliated clubs
- School executive leadership team development
- Spiritual/cultural leadership
- Risk management and compliance
- Philanthropy and fundraising
- Finance and resource management
- Organisation-wide management and administration
- Community leadership and engagement
- Pedagogical leadership
- Instructional leadership.

It can help to have a few of these skills as well:

- Grit, resilience and toughness
- Empathy
- Self-belief
- Judgement
- Determination
- Interpersonal and commuication
- Integrity and honour.

SCHOOLS ARE BUSINESSES

A snapshot of the size and complexity of independent schools in Australia shows they are medium-large businesses.

Across the spectrum of the 1100+ independent schools in Australia, some have gross recurrent income ranging from less than $10M in smaller schools to well in excess of $20M, and in some cases $50M (ISCA, 2020).

Melbourne Grammar School generates more than $75M in total income. Sydney Grammar School generates more than $90M. There are dozens and dozens of schools across the country with budgets of this scale.

Independent schools have enrolments ranging from fewer than 50 students to schools with more than 2000 pupils. Caulfield Grammar has over 3000 students; Haileybury College has over 4000. This means that there could be more than 10,000 people in these communities. The average independent school in Australia has 500 students, as part of a small community of close to 2000.

Independent schools employ fewer than twenty teaching and non-teaching staff in some cases, to more than 500 in other cases. Barker College in Sydney has close to 1000 staff.

Operating surplus (profit) is crucial in independent schools. While managing a school takes passion and people skills, you also require a stable source of funds to secure the school's finances. It is vitally important that you generate sufficient funds to:

- Meet salary and wages costs – a school of 500 students, with 90 staff and a budget of $12M, could have wages costs of $9M – or 75 per cent of the operational expenditure
- Meet borrowing costs on loans for capital development
- Cover depreciation of buildings, assets, plant and equipment
- Cover the costs of new buildings and asset development, reinvesting in the school
- Meet tuition expenses and student activities
- Cover administration costs, including electricity, consumables, insurance (including Workcover)
- Cover marketing and communications (independent schools are in a competitive market)
- Keep up with information, communications and technology infrastructure and services
- Cover buildings and grounds expenses
- Meet recruitment costs.

Your value proposition has to be clear and your point of difference to your competitors has to be visible. Much of that is to do with the presentation of your campus. This is only possible if you turn your budget into a profit, every year.

If you are unable to generate the funds you need to cut it with your competitors, then it is likely that you will have to close down your school. A school needs to achieve a certain level of profitability to deliver its basic promise: to provide quality education and an environment conducive to learning.

Your reputation is priceless. Your business is education, and you need a strong customer service paradigm as well. How parents would talk positively about their child's school can be likened to how a satisfied customer would recommend a certain restaurant to their friends. I have come to know that a school's reputation depends on how parents perceive the school. Are they happy with what their kids learn and achieve? Are they content with the facilities and services provided to them? If so, then parents will most likely spread the word and provide credible testimonials based on their experience. This is business.

Simpson (2021) writing in *The Australian Financial Review* claimed that:

> ... *big schools are big businesses and need to be run accordingly. Going further to add that its time educators saw it as such and ceased their preciousness over the issue.*

Knowing the key financial benchmarks

There is so much to learn about the financial management of a school. Chances are you will need to build the financial acumen you need. Your business manager will know the numbers, the business model and key financial data in great detail, but you have to be able to read the important numbers. If you can get your hands on your own financials, ask your business manager to explain the following, and the industry benchmarks for schools of your size and operational budget:

- Cash flow adequacy
- Net cash from operations
- Minimum working capital
- Reinvestment
- Interest cover
- Debt per student
- Total recurrent income per student
- Discounts and concessions as a per cent of total fee income
- Teacher salaries per student

- Net operating margin
- Student/teacher ratios.

There are many indicators you could review to keep an eye on the school's financial health – the above is indicative only. Don't despair if your financial understanding is lacking, or you feel in over your depth – there are organisations that support schools with this sort of analysis.

BOARDS EXPECT THE PRINCIPAL TO BE A CEO

The boards of large, autonomous independent schools in Australia regard their principals as CEOs and expect them to perform as such. As part of my work now, I support aspiring principals apply to principal positions. An examination of the recruitment prospectuses used for the appointment of independent school principals in these schools found CEO to be a commonly used term. Here are some examples:

> The Principal is the CEO of Townsville Grammar School and responsible to the Board of Trustees for the overall leadership and management of the three campuses of the School. (Townsville Grammar School, 2017, p 11)

> The Principal is the Chief Executive Officer and is responsible to the Board for the strategic direction and operational leadership of Queenwood. (Queenwood School for Girls, 2013, p 6)

There is no ambiguity here, this is the expectation – principals in independent schools are regarded as the CEO.

Despite many principals' reluctance to be compared to a CEO, the boards of independent schools in Australia expect the principal to run the school like a business or corporation. The bottom line is financial viability and future-proofing the school.

Boards expect that their principals will take up membership of relevant professional associations such as the local chapter of The CEO Institute and AICD. Boards may ask principals to complete such courses as the AICD Company Directors Course or others through the Australian Institute of Management, or even Harvard Business School.

If principals don't meet the expectations of their boards and learn to become effective CEOs, their tenure will be short! There is nothing that the independent school principal is not responsible for and held accountable for.

During the case study research as part of my thesis, a colleague explained that the corporatisation of independent school boards has resulted in the average tenure of an independent school principal falling to three years. That squarely reflects the corporate world with its revolving door approach to CEO tenure.

As in the corporate world, principals in independent schools sign a formal contract with the board, which stipulates the terms and conditions of appointment; duties and responsibilities; the principal's relationship with the board; remuneration and salary benefits; performance review and appraisal; termination of employment procedures; and other contractual matters.

Here is the termination clause from the standard contract for an independent school principal. Despite signing a three- or five-year contract, this clause effectively makes it a six-month contract. This extract is taken from my own contract for my second principalship.

28.   Termination of Engagement by the School

28.1   The Board may terminate the Principal's Engagement with the School at any time by giving to the Principal six-months written notice (or pay in lieu of notice).

To assist the principal's longer-term tenure, which is desirable in my view, it is important to have rigorous performance appraisals. Most principals' contracts are five years. I found it worked best to have appraisals at the end of the first year and early in the fourth year. It was helpful to me to get quite explicit feedback about my performance after the first year. Feedback with actions for improved performance meant I could apply myself earnestly in the second and third years. My contracts were five-year contracts, so I would seek a contract extension in my fourth year. Given this timing, I was always happy to have a rigorous review conducted prior to commencing negotiations for a new contract. It is desirable that these reviews be conducted by someone external to the school, who is experienced in principalship in independent schools and well versed in the demands of the role.

Surviving your term really means attending to the formal and informal elements of your contract. There are lots of indicators and measures at the disposal of boards to assess the performance of the principal, the one that seems to bubble to the surface most often is community engagement and managing relationships. Parent, staff and student satisfaction with you plays a role in this.

As part of my thesis, I developed a leadership framework for principals leading large, P–12, autonomous, independent schools in Australia:

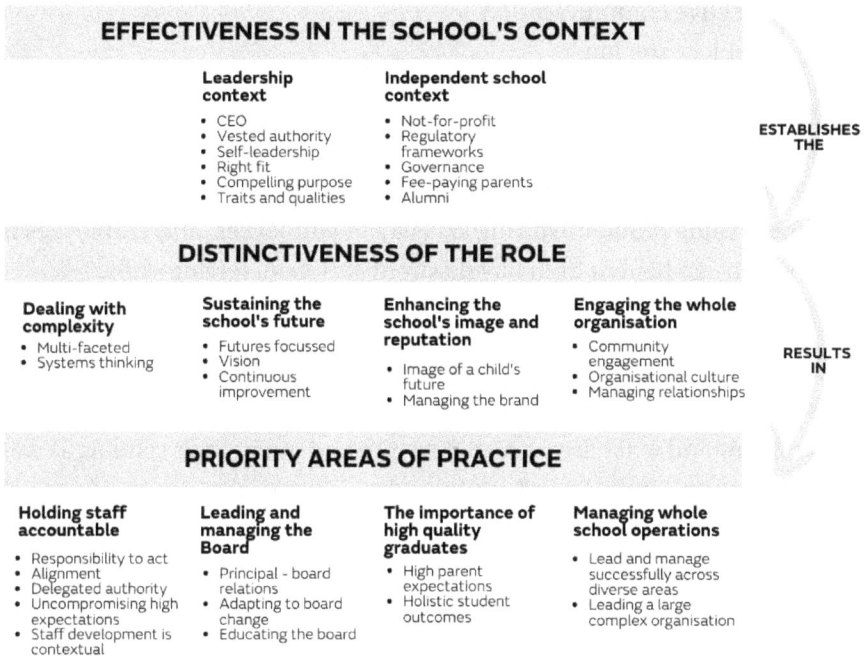

EFFECTIVENESS IN THE SCHOOL'S CONTEXT

Leadership context
- CEO
- Vested authority
- Self-leadership
- Right fit
- Compelling purpose
- Traits and qualities

Independent school context
- Not-for-profit
- Regulatory frameworks
- Governance
- Fee-paying parents
- Alumni

ESTABLISHES THE

DISTINCTIVENESS OF THE ROLE

Dealing with complexity
- Multi-faceted
- Systems thinking

Sustaining the school's future
- Futures focussed
- Vision
- Continuous improvement

Enhancing the school's image and reputation
- Image of a child's future
- Managing the brand

Engaging the whole organisation
- Community engagement
- Organisational culture
- Managing relationships

RESULTS IN

PRIORITY AREAS OF PRACTICE

Holding staff accountable
- Responsibility to act
- Alignment
- Delegated authority
- Uncompromising high expectations
- Staff development is contextual

Leading and managing the Board
- Principal - board relations
- Adapting to board change
- Educating the board

The importance of high quality graduates
- High parent expectations
- Holistic student outcomes

Managing whole school operations
- Lead and manage successfully across diverse areas
- Leading a large complex organisation

Business Acumen

I believe that principals need business acumen skills to succeed in their role as a CEO. A person with strong business acumen understands various aspects of the school and how it's run as a business, and can then make competent decisions based on this knowledge.

The following form a set of business acumen skills that are worth working on:

- Time management
- Organisation
- Innovation
- Delegation
- Strategic thinking
- Market orientation
- Analytical skills
- Marketing skills
- Effective communication
- Problem solving.

Problem-solving skills refer to a person's ability to handle unexpected or challenging situations in an effective way. Strong problem-solving skills allow individuals to determine the source of an issue and come to a viable solution. Employers value problem-solving skills in all employees, and employees in any position can benefit from having strong problem-solving skills.

Financial acumen – a principal's financial literacy and ability to understand processes related to reporting, budgeting, forecasting and other financial skills – is another key element that contributes to business acumen. Principals must understand what drives cash flow into and out of their schools as well as how to maximise profit and minimise loss. Financial acumen refers to all aspects of a school's monetary transactions and economic value; it allows leaders to better understand and manage financial indicators related to stakeholders, resources, goals and market success.

So, how do you improve your business acumen skills?

1. Get to know your school's business model
2. Understand the financial side of the school
3. Invest in your own learning and development to strengthen your business acumen
4. Find a mentor who is a CEO.

Professional isolation

As an independent school principal, I had to deal with professional isolation. I was fortunate that the board had vested authority in me, but this often resulted in me leading on my own – the decisions I had to make could have a direct impact on a staff member, a group of staff where structural changes had to be made, parents and groups of parents. Decisions had to be made about the viability of a school and this was not something I could speak of openly with staff and parents.

A principal in a government or systemic Catholic school has the support of a governing educational system to address, for example, legal, financial, maintenance and building development issues. This is not the case for an independent school principal.

Professional isolation will be something you have to deal with. This is where professional associations and colleague principals in other schools were of great benefit to me. A peer mentor relationship worked well for colleagues and for me. One of the best antidotes for me was regular professional development. I also found that getting out of my own school and visiting colleagues in other schools helped, to see that we deal with the same general issues.

In hindsight

Despite their reluctance to accept the likeness, the responsibilities of the independent school principal (in Australia) are akin to a CEO in a not-for-profit company. It cannot be denied. The boards of autonomous, independent schools in Australia regard their principals as CEOs and expect them to perform as such.

Independent schools in Australia are run like any business or corporation. If a principal cannot perform in the role of CEO, they cannot be effective; indeed, they will not survive in the role if they cannot. To perform at the level of CEO, principals must acquire appropriate expertise to run their schools effectively as businesses/corporations. Anecdotally, principals in independent schools have not warmed to this concept, instead preferring their role to be deemed as educational leader.

Because independent school principals lead schools, they do pay attention to pedagogy, teaching and learning, teacher development, instruction, and assessment. However, they delegate this responsibility to executive leaders in their schools while never straying too far from the discourse and conversations. The fact is, they are running a business – and generating a surplus is a priority.

LEADING AND MANAGING THE BOARD

Independent school boards

What distinguishes independent schools from other non-government schools is their independence, or autonomy of operation within legislated boundaries. Independent schools are set up and governed on an individual school basis, connected directly to their community and answerable to their own governing board or management committee. A comprehensive range of accountabilities to parents, governments and other stakeholders exists in independent schools.

What does that mean for the principal? It means the buck stops with you. There is nothing that you are not responsible for. This was an outcome clearly demonstrated by my doctoral studies.

Independent school boards delegate the responsibility for running the school to the principal and, in exchange, hold them accountable for their school's overall performance and sustainability. Independent school boards take an active and keen interest in the day-to-day management activities and whole-school operations because of the ensuing impact on the board's legal and fiduciary responsibilities.

Because these school boards are set up as companies under the regulations of the Australian Securities & Investments Commission (ASIC), directors assume significant legal and financial risk. They therefore want to be informed of how the organisation is being managed to ensure all legal obligations are being met. This introduces a layer of accountability and responsibility which is simply not present in government schools and systemic Catholic schools, where the principal can rely on the system to support the school. The principals who took part in my doctoral case studies do enjoy autonomy, but this creates another tension – they are fully accountable for every aspect of the school's operation. This is good while everything is going well, but it can cause undue stress and tension if there is a hiccup.

Where boards are over-zealous, the principal can end up being disrupted and micro-managed by the board. Where boards don't understand governance, rogue directors can interfere in operational matters – they either think they can do better than management or they are over-eager in carrying out their fiduciary responsibility.

Most Australian independent schools are separately incorporated as not-for-profit companies limited by guarantee. These legal entities are public companies governed by a board of directors – sometimes referred to as a school council. In order to receive federal funding, independent schools are registered as not-for-profit institutions and comply with the wide-ranging and detailed legislative requirements of the Australian Education Act 2013.

A not-for-profit school in Australia is a school that does not operate for the profit, personal gain, or other benefit for individuals, for example, the principal, directors, or fee-paying parents. They can make a profit, called a surplus, but any profit made must be used in pursuing the school's purposes and objectives and keeping the school running.

One of the most significant capital projects I completed when I was a principal – with the help of a friend and colleague, who at the time was the director of development – was a $6M concert hall and music centre, with fundraising of over $2M. In the 2020s, there are independent schools that have building projects of $20M, $30M and more. The achievement above was in 2005, and the tuition fee for a year 12 student was $10,000. Our annual operational budget was just over $10M. It was a gargantuan effort.

Some independent schools have been subject to intense scrutiny by government because they were operating for profit, in some cases distributing profits to directors and paying large amounts of money to director-owned companies, without that company providing any service. Fortunately, this doesn't happen very often, and when it does it is like the circus has come to town.

In 2019 Queensland police arrested the former principal of a private Logan school and three of his family members — charging them with significant fraud offences over the financial management of the school between 2012 and 2018. It was alleged at the time that $4.6M of college money had been taken and used for items including luxury holidays over a seven-year period.

The former financial controller of a wealthy eastern suburbs school in 2019 was investigated for fraud. The financial controller managed the school's money for more than fifteen years, and in the middle of the investigation had his assets frozen after an application by the school to the NSW Supreme Court. The college had to retain legal and forensic advisors in respect of the suspected fraud.

These are very serious issues for a school community and an independent school board. The governance arrangements in independent schools do leave them vulnerable to this sort of activity, and schools need highly effective internal and external systems of control, supervision, and audit to ensure this doesn't happen.

One extension of managing the board is management of meetings and the political nature of committees. Aspirants do need to learn early in the piece that there doesn't have to be a committee for everything, and forming a sub-committee to make a decision may not be the best approach. Sometimes committees are formed to provide the CEO with support to get an idea actualised. I would rally against this as a model of decision making. Your executive team are in place to make important decisions about the school's operations and innovation/change; additional committees can muddy this water and make things unnecessarily convoluted.

Board expectations

Just to illustrate how invidious it can be as a principal in an independent school – where you have a contract and a local board that can wield unchecked power, putting your tenure on shaky ground – I recount what happened to a colleague and good friend of mine. Kelvin (not his real name) called me one day to ask for my advice. He said his board was moving on him and he feared they would dismiss him. He believed it was because a small number of under-performing executive staff were not happy with his introduction of a tough performance-management regime.

Sure enough, the board engaged in their own kangaroo court and terminated Kelvin without notice. Fortunately, Kelvin was able to rally the support of the Church hierarchy and kept his job.

In a school where the local board had no accountability, the principal would be marched out of his/her office, network access blocked, and communications frozen. The only option for the unfairly dismissed principal would be a long, protracted and costly legal battle that would not achieve reinstatement but might result in some financial settlement.

Boards of independent schools in Australia have clear, shared understandings about what they want in their CEOs, as shown in the table here:

Expectations held for independent school principals by school boards	Traits and qualitites required by independent school principals
When I read the prospectuses for the recruitment of independent school principals, I found consistency across all schools about the core expectations.	As part of the quantitative research done using a self-completion online questionnaire, principals reported that they needed these traits and qualities.
CEO	Integrity
Governance and board relations	Good judgement
Strategic/visionary leadership	Resilience
Educational leader	Drive and stamina
Pedagogical leader	Inspiring
Curriculum leader	Self-confidence
Student engagement and wellbeing	Passion for education
Staff leadership, development and wellbeing	Inter-personal and communicaiton skills
Community leadership and engagement	Empathy
Organisation management and administration	Delegation skills
Finance and resource management	Positivity
Philanthropy and fundraising	Sense of humour
Risk management and compliance	Self-learner
Spiritual/cultural leadership	Moral courage
School executive leadership team development	Openess
Human resource management	Decision making skills
Marketing and public relations	
Christian leader (in Christian schools)	

The role of independent school principal is a complex and demanding one, at times, unbearable. Having said that, it is one of the most noble and fulfilling roles that anyone could attain.

The autonomy of independent schools in Australia brings significant responsibilities for the principal, none more important and demanding as the relationship of integrity that exists between the school and the students and families it serves. Within this context, principals must be accountable to their school community through the school board. This context for principalship is quite exclusive in this country, and this makes the role of the independent school principal in Australia quite unique.

Independent school boards present the principal with somewhat of a dilemma. Due to funding arrangements with the commonwealth government, directors on independent school boards are not allowed to be paid; they must be voluntary. This creates a problem because independent schools find it hard to attract professional directors, directors from outside their own communities. Boards made up of members of the community, parents, directors from local church groups and community groups can lack corporate nous. They can struggle to establish effective governance principles, practices and behaviours.

To overcome this, the principal must be instrumental in seeing that the board is subject to external reviews – not just the navel-gazing, self-appraisal type of reviews that are commonly trumpeted. The board should undergo rigorous external review every two years, by a professional organisation that works with not-for-profit and for-profit boards.

The principal and the chair must see that rogue directors are removed. They must ensure that the school has a skills-based board that adds value to the governance and leadership of the school. Sometimes, the chair is the problem!

Boards play a significant part in the governance of our schools. They have the potential to add much value to the development of our schools. At the same time, they have the potential to disrupt in destructive ways. Good leadership and management of schools can be thrown off track if the board steps out of its lane and tries to micro-manage the operations of the school. I don't say this to create undue anxiety or to misrepresent the good work that boards can do – but it is all too common, especially with the community-type boards largely composed of parents and, in some cases, teachers.

Board reviews

I am often asked by principals how often a board should have a performance review.

Most independent schools are not obliged to assess their performance at all. Some boards do not evaluate their performance, to the detriment of good governance in these schools. Others conduct reviews on an "as needs" basis, sometimes triggered by changes to board composition and new directors asking the question, or in response to known poor board performance.

I recommend that boards conduct a major review every two years. Schools are dynamic environments and changes occur relatively frequently. A more extensive process can be adopted when an external facilitator is involved. It is important that independent school boards govern with responsibility, professionalism and to ensure the long-term viability of the school. External reviews are an important part of ensuring this.

Know this from the outset: do not be complacent when it comes to your board. This can be your undoing, and you can be completely blindsided by it. Do not ever be self-satisfied in this part of the role. I have heard principals tell me on one day that they have a great relationship with their board, only to have that turn on its head when an influential parent decides they don't like a decision the principal has made. I had a member of my staff who did not like my high standards and exacting expectations, and they made a complaint to the board about bullying and harassment. I don't like the phrase "it went pear-shaped", but things can go that way, and so easily. The situation I found myself in was stressful and it took a long time to be resolved. Disparaging or malicious allegations are difficult to disprove or shake off.

The board has significant impact on your autonomy and authority, and the challenges associated with its management cannot be under-estimated. The board is in place to ensure the principal as CEO meets all the obligations expected of the school as a company.

It is your role to see that appropriate training and development is provided to the board directors. You do this with the backing and assistance of the board chair. Just as the principal is expected to run the school as a CEO and as a business, directors must understand the requirements on them to see that the school meets its financial imperatives. The board has stewardship for the school's operations and outcomes.

The relationship between board and principal

A point well made by one of the case study principals was that, unlike a CEO in the private sector, a principal is required to meet face-to-face with stakeholders on a daily basis. He said, "You can't get access to the CEO of Qantas, Alan Joyce, no matter how hard you try." The point being made here is that parents expect to be able to communicate directly with the principal and get access to the principal, and directors – in the schools I have led – expect the same. Either at board meetings or via email or personal appointment, they expect access to the principal to raise concerns, ideas or share their own thoughts and perspectives, which the principal is obliged to take on board. You carry the weight of expectation of an entire community. Another case-study principal said, "You are on call continuously, carrying the expectations of every one of your community, and then those agencies outside of the school."

The relationship between the principal and the board is at its best when directors know and are aware that management of a school is delegated to the principal. This can be a source of tension, usually when a board has inexperienced directors, directors are drawn from, or represent, "interest" stakeholders, or where governance departs from contemporary governance principles and practices into community-minded association governance traits. It is important that the board charter establishes boundaries and delegates proper authority to the principal.

The principal, like the CEO, implements the strategy approved by the board and ensures that the organisation's structure and processes meet the strategic and cultural needs of the organisation (AHISA, 2011).

From my experience, the board charter should delegate authority to the principal in these areas:

- To speak on behalf of the school, representing the school in the media
- To seek legal advice on behalf of the school
- To set salaries
- To hire and fire staff
- To manage student suspensions and exclusions
- To manage key appointments, including business manager, chaplain, deputy, heads of school, etc. The board may want to have a board member sit on the selection panel, but the authority must remain with the principal.

The principal's remuneration is a contentious issue in most schools. I have seen the full board involved in the principal's salary, both at the time of appointment and at periodic reviews. This is not a good model. The best model I have seen is where the chair, deputy chair and finance director form a panel to oversee this.

The board may expect the principal to engage with it in developing, implementing, and monitoring the mission and vision for the school. Let me tell you that this is something you must lead. You don't need the board for this – this is your job. You design and sustain the culture that you want. Forget what the website says, or the objectives of the company; you set the mission and vision for the school. How you do it is the trick. You must know your school's context, the parent demography and expectations, the school's resources, assets and aspirations. Get ahead of your board on this one. Plan the school's future. Take your key executive with you.

One of my colleagues had to take measures to have board members removed because they weren't supporting the culture he valued. "This time last year I got rid of three board members in one hit. So, three board members causing me trouble, and at the end of the day if the board didn't support me, I was prepared to walk."

A director didn't like the direction the principal was taking on a particular strategic objective. The director enlisted the backing of two other directors and began a campaign of community talk about the principal, undermining trust and confidence in him. My colleague wasn't going to stand for this, so he asked the chair to take decisive action against the rogue directors, cautioning that if appropriate action wasn't taken, the principal would resign. Common sense prevailed and the principal remained in office.

Another colleague had taken decisive action against some executive leaders for under-performance. The executive leaders drew on support from their friends on the board and began a campaign to destabilise the board's support for the principal. They were successful. The mischief-making directors rallied the chair and sufficient directors to have my colleague's contract terminated. My colleague, after taking advice from the state-based association of independent schools, went to the church and the governing body, and had the decision of the board over-turned. And the entire board was dismissed.

Don't allow yourself to be subservient to your board.

Boards often want to insert key performance indicators into the annual reviews of principals' performance. Resist this. Push back. It is problematic to measure the success of schools – a lot of the things you do in a school can't be measured. If you want students to have generosity of spirit, you can't measure that. Or if you want your graduates to be good people, good citizens – you can't measure that.

Dr David Mulford (2018) claimed that:

> ...there is a growth in demand by school boards for measuring outcomes, to define key performance indicators of principals and senior staff, to create challenging benchmarks, to demonstrate value add for parents paying fees and to validate to parents why they should send their son or daughter to an independent school.

> That accountability trend is right and proper. School boards and principals need a framework from which to start meaningful conversations around the measurement of success of their particular school. The challenge is that so much of what principals do in schools obstinately refuses to allow itself to be measured.

> Difficulties can arise when educators who come from a non-business background seek to get consensus on success indicators from board members who may come from the business world that is used to metrics and clear performance indicators. Soft edges can clash with hard edges. Complexities of a "people" industry can clash with a

perceived lack of improved accountability measures for teachers. Where is the agreed area between hard metrics and the complex world of educating five-to-eighteen-year-olds? This is a world full of so many variables. A school is a human construct where the development of the human spirit can most appropriately defy accurate measurement.

Because most independent school boards are set up as companies under the regulations of ASIC, directors assume significant legal and risk responsibilities. Consequently, they want to be informed of how the organisation is being managed to ensure all their legal and fiduciary obligations are being met. While the boards I have worked with (and this is generally the case in independent schools) have delegated the responsibility for running the school to me as principal, in exchange, they held me accountable for school's performance. But they certainly took an active and keen interest in the day-to-day management activities and whole school operations.

This introduced a layer of accountability and responsibility for me to contend with, and at times was oppressive and debilitating. I did enjoy autonomy, but it created another tension – I was fully accountable for my school's total performance in every aspect of the school's operation, and I couldn't delegate this.

The principal's relationship with the school board and the challenges associated with managing it, along with the impact that the board has on the autonomy and authority of the principal, produce significant issues for principals that need careful negotiation and management. Indeed, this is one area of the role that requires constant vigilance on the part of the principal.

Boards in independent schools can create serious problems for principals when an immature or power-hungry board want to involve themselves in the daily operations of the school. They may put their principals under heavy scrutiny. When this happens, it compromises the governance-operations principles that must be preserved for effective leadership and management. This is all too common in independent schools in Australia.

The relationship between a principal and the board is critical to the success of a school; a positive, productive relationship between the board and the principal is an enabler for effective principal leadership. It is worth putting time and effort into this relationship; if you don't, it could be perilous, impacting on your tenure.

There is a residual risk for principals in independent schools should the board chair change, or the makeup of the board change. When this happens, the principal's leadership traits, qualities and practices may no longer be the right fit for board members. The principal must draw on their agility and adaptability to deal with this challenge. This is the tenuous nature of the principal's appointment in an autonomous, independent school.

Another challenge can arise when the board expects the principal to do certain things that do not align with the principal's own values and beliefs or, indeed, are unethical. Responses to situations of this kind are quite critical for the principal's relationship with their board. When this happens, the principal must manage this with diplomacy and tact, drawing on all their intellect and social competence. To navigate these murky waters, principals need strong collegial network support and expert advice from the professional associations that support principals. Do not be idle when such problems surface, or the result will be a short tenure.

Unfortunately, there are cases where the board's direction might not be consistent with the direction the principal is taking the school in. The principal must manage this situation without fracturing the relationship. This is best managed with the board chair; the chair has an important role to play in assisting and supporting the principal. The dynamic relationship between the chair and the principal brings positive support and value to the principal's role.

Unfortunately, it is (poor) board behaviour that has contributed to the demise of many independent school principals, and this persists as one of the most significant areas of concern to principalship in independent schools. This can be mitigated by a strong, productive and mutually respectful relationship between the board chair and the principal.

All boards should confer with their principal to make a particular decision in conjunction with the principal; the principal then must put the decision into effect based on the legislative, registration and school policy requirements. Boards should not intervene in the management of the school. This is the role of the principal. Don't wait for the board to take this lead – you must manage this for the outcome that you want.

Relationship between chair and CEO

The relationship between the chair and CEO is critical. I like the "no surprises" role for the board chair. This is where the principal is not blindsided at board meetings by matters being raised without notice. There should be no surprises for the principal, allowing them to give proper time and attention to any matters that might be on the agenda or raised at a board meeting.

I felt it was important that my relationship with the chair should be professional, oriented towards the business of the school, friendly and affable. I strove to have professional and personal trust and respect be mutual. The best chairs, for me, were those who could act as a mentor or sounding board for me. We enjoyed a relationship of frankness and candour (behind the scenes) and unity and mutual support (in public).

The schools I have been involved with have been at their best when the chair and principal worked together on challenges and uncertainty. In these cases, the main channel of communication between the board and management between board meetings was through the chair and the principal.

I was expected to meet with the chair from time to time between board meetings to help set board agendas, to debrief following board meetings and to exchange updates and give guidance on issues affecting the school. These principles worked extremely well in my last school.

> *There has to be a close relationship between the principal and the chair which is collaborative, and professional, with mutual understanding and respect to ensure the effective functioning of the school and the ability to manage unforeseen events. (Governance Institute of Australia, 2015, p 15)*

The principal's board report

A successful and productive relationship between the school board and the principal is critical to ensure the best outcomes and decisions emerge from board deliberations. In turn, such decisions may affect the work of the staff, student learning outcomes, and the educational environment of the school.

The principal should attend all board meetings. Sessions where the principal is excluded from discussions should be kept to an absolute minimum. One such acceptable situation is when the principal's salary and benefits are being discussed.

I have written over 200 board reports for four different boards. I learned over the years that it is best practice to restrict reports to the formal cycle of board meetings and not venture too often to writing to the board "out of session." I suggest that the principal should report on these matters:

- The implementation of future planning and strategy
- Significant changes in education that will impact the school; for example, changes to the ATAR
- Student achievement and progress, including Year 12 academic results
- Co-curricular performance and student leadership and service activities
- Staff development, learning and retention
- Enrolment levels and enrolment sustainability
- Fundraising, donations, and relationships with external stakeholders and corporate partnerships
- Financial performance
- Policy, legal, risk and compliance matters
- Parent, staff, and student satisfaction levels (using survey instruments)
- Wellbeing and pastoral care of staff and students
- Parent and community activities.

While this is not an exhaustive list of themes that can be reported to the board, it does highlight how important it is to keep the board informed through the principal's regular report. Some boards meet monthly, others less frequently. One of my boards met every six weeks.

In hindsight

As a principal in an independent school in Australia, you are the CEO – don't let anyone else tell you differently. With the board, you set the mission and vision – you drive the process, but the board must sign off.

Part of being CEO is to be the chief education officer too. In your preparation for being a principal and early in your principalship, do as much reading as you can about CEOs from the corporate world. I really enjoyed reading Brené Brown's *Dare to Lead*; Gail Kelly's *Live, Lead, Learn*, Richard Branson's *The Virgin Way*, and anything about Nelson Mandela, Winston Churchill or Abraham Lincoln. I read lots about the corporate, political, and business world. That's where I lived. The AICD is an excellent resource for principals, and I recommend membership. This is where you can learn about boards, and gain a myriad of understandings about governance. Annual membership costs less than $1000 and is well worth it.

At the end of the day, make sure there is a clear, shared understanding of what governance is, and how it works in reality. Make sure you have an open, transparent relationship with your board chair. Make sure that you get an opportunity, at least every six months, to clarify expectations between the board and you as the principal. Make sure you have a professional relationship with your board that gives you the appropriate status, authority and autonomy to run the school, and also affords the professional respect to have a say in the training, development, and performance of the board.

ACCOUNTABILITY

Conflict between two staff members can cause you and your school so much grief. Make sure it is a responsibility you keep inside your portfolio. You must be prepared to act if staff do not toe the line. High expectations of staff in independent schools are a given, but that is not sufficient. You will need to have robust accountability frameworks to ensure that staff comply with your direction and that they perform to your standard. This is where courage comes into the game – do you have the courage to challenge teachers if they are not doing all they can for the learning, growth and wellbeing of students? Do you have the courage to speak candidly to a non-teaching member of staff if their conduct toward a colleague is inconsistent with the school's values?

The case-study principals that I interviewed all held high expectations of their staff, and they had robust accountability frameworks to ensure that staff complied and performed.

Each of the case-study principals described how they had the courage to challenge teachers if they were not doing all they could for the learning, growth and wellbeing of students. They knew it was their job to see that staff are aligned with the direction that the school was headed. They were prepared to act where and when they needed to.

This didn't always go well of course. I have countless stories of where I had to act with a staff member who was not meeting the standard and who was not prepared to support the values and beliefs of the school. The most hazardous part of the job is when there is conflict between two members of staff; this is often brushed aside as a personality conflict but can become a serious issue for all concerned.

Managing challenging HR matters is the responsibility of the principal. In some schools, where a HR manager is in place, the principal would work closely with them to manage these situations.

I had one situation late in my career where a head of department (HoD) felt threatened by a new appointment to her department. It started out as a simple complaint and ended in a full-blown investigation by an external agency. The HoD had been on the interview panel and endorsed the decision to appoint the new teacher, who was an experienced, highly respected teacher across the state-based professional associations.

From the very commencement of the new teacher's term at our school, the HoD engaged in a steady and sure campaign of bullying and intimidation. It was furtive, but nonetheless effective and demoralising for the new teacher. Colleagues observed it and brought it to my attention. It turned into a protracted drama playing out over a year. Incredibly, the board involved themselves, and even the newly appointed HR manager weighed in. It was a terribly divisive situation.

I addressed the matter early. I didn't let it fester but tried to diffuse the situation before it escalated. I didn't do this personally; I used the appropriate senior staff to try and manage the situation. That wasn't successful, because my senior staff didn't have the skills or experience to deal with the depth and intensity of this arduous conflict. My senior staff members certainly applied their time and effort, and they were diligent. It wasn't for the lack of trying that this didn't work.

Next, I brought the staff in conflict together, using mediation methods to allow each staff member to voice their concerns. I encouraged each person to come with a solution-based approach. I stuck with this for a few months, allowing the staff to work with me and senior staff to address concerns and issues in an ethical way.

Progress was not being made, so I engaged a qualified and experienced external mediator with dispute and conflict resolution skills. The mediator was involved for about three months, which included two full-day visits to the school to work with the aggrieved staff. At the end of the period the mediator advised me the situation was unresolvable because neither party would move from their position. I knew then that I would have to go to a formal investigation, which I did. The investigation found what we expected: both parties had a role to play in the deterioration of the workplace relationship and would need to take an active role in restoring the relationship. The two staff members kept working together but they had an intense dislike for each other.

Holding staff accountable has four factors associated with it: your responsibility to act when staff are not supporting the school or their colleagues; aligning staff to the vision, values and beliefs of the school; holding uncompromising high expectations of staff; and judicious delegating.

Responsibility to act

In each of my roles I had significant work to do to lead, develop and align staff across all areas of the school's operations. I knew if they didn't comply, they would expose our school to significant reputational, legal and compliance risk and put my own tenure at risk.

I had to learn how to lead and develop my staff and hold them accountable for their commitment to the school's strategic direction and goals and aspirations. This is not something that comes naturally. You have to learn how to manage this part of the role, take on appropriate training, seek the counsel of wise colleagues, collaborate with your executive team, even use a coach.

During the case-study interviews, a central theme ran through the conversations; the case-study principals required their staff to perform at high levels and to support the direction, plans and aspirations that they had for the school. There was a clear expectation held by these principals that staff would be committed.

This involved providing robust and authoritative leadership within a collegial approach to working with executive and middle leaders.

In the case of my executive leaders, who reported directly to me, there is a tension that exists between autonomy and supervision. I was prepared to delegate decision making and authority to executive team members who had responsibilities for different aspects of the organisation, yet I knew I had to stay close to the decision-making processes of my executive leaders, providing wisdom, counsel and direction if needed.

You will find yourself embroiled in some bizarre staff matters that you never thought could happen. I had one such, and still to this day shake my head and wonder if it really happened.

Many independent schools have end-of-year functions, sponsored by the school board, to thank and celebrate the work of staff. At one such dinner, catered for by professional caterers, around 225 staff, partners and directors gathered in our hall. Of course, at events of this kind, there was some alcohol consumed.

I was about to leave for the evening when the event manager came over to me, agitated and stressed. She told me that a staff member was loading alcohol into the boot of his car, helping himself to the remnants of the evening. Without a moment's hesitation I marched off to the carpark.

There I found the staff member's partner and eighteen-year-old son – who had come to pick him up – waiting patiently inside the car while the staff member loaded the boot. He wasn't taking one or two bottles, he had helped himself to a carton and a half. Unbelievable! Of course, I intervened. He didn't return to our school. But it did require a protracted process that involved mediation with the Fair Work Commission (FWC).

Forming friendships with staff and work colleagues

Forming personal friendships in the workplace is a high-risk activity.

It becomes difficult for you to give tough feedback. Inevitably you will be called to act on an issue of under-performance or matter of concern with the staff member who has become a friend.

Information shared between people cannot be taken back, and sometimes, it may adversely work against you.

There may be accusations of favouritism from other staff who do not have a friendship with you.

Just don't put yourself in that position. Make sure you maintain faithful, loyal friendships with friends outside of your organisation.

Moving people on

There will likely come a point when you realise a staff member is not a good fit – they are clearly under-performing, they are not providing a service to their business partners in the school, you are paying them a lot of money for little return. You won't need a performance review to know this, you will know – and your staff will be telling you to get rid of them.

When considering the ultimate decision, always revert to what is best for the students. You can't compromise the quality of children's learning, and if a teacher can't cut the mustard, they have to go.

If you decide to terminate a staff member's employment for poor performance, there are HR processes that you need to follow to ensure you don't unfairly dismiss somebody. In short, the basic process is: an informal chat; a formal discussion; the school's disciplinary process; a verbal warning; a written warning; a final written warning; and termination. This can be time consuming, costly, and stressful for all.

The best way to terminate an employee with the least pain and cost is to make their role redundant. This is reasonably straightforward and providing you follow the principles that support redundancy, you should be protected from unfair dismissal claims and a lengthy Fair Work Commission process. There are some important considerations to take into account.

Engage a legal firm early in the piece to provide the steps required, the formal correspondence and a script for discussions. Legal advice is an imperative if you haven't had the experience before. An employment lawyer can also provide you with the confidence that you are doing the right thing.

If the employee adds value to the overall performance of the school and is generally aligned and a good fit, but just not suited for the role they have, find another suitable role in the school for them. It is also a mark of respect for your staff to find alternatives to dismissal.

Alignment

One thing that can cost you credibility and cause staff to withdraw support and trust is lack of transparency. If your staff believe you are withholding information or not acting openly, they will begin to question your decisions. Often, you are not even aware of this happening. I knew that transparency was critical for staff to see the work behind the scenes and understand the motives behind decisions. If you hope to achieve staff alignment with your vision and strategy be sure to be open and transparent.

There is significant work to be done by a principal to ensure that staff working in different sections across the enterprise are focused on the same ends. Staff need to see and appreciate the connections and alignment that are needed for whole school effectiveness.

As a principal I was judged by the work I did with staff to ensure they were committed to the culture, aspirations, vision and values that I had set for the school and put into place. I don't think we should kid ourselves; boards don't do that – principals do!

My research found that the role of principal in large, P–12, autonomous, independent schools in Australia has less to do with the detail of pedagogy, teaching and learning, and more to do with leading and developing staff at a more corporate level.

During my research, I observed my colleague principals watching and interacting with staff in meetings and when walking about their schools. I could see the deliberate role modelling, teaching and coaching that they provided. Their conversations were purposeful opportunities to reinforce the principal's expectations. I observed the principals articulate what they wanted to achieve to garner staff alignment to the principal's aspirations and goals. I witnessed them take every opportunity to articulate their purpose for the school, and to build the staff's alignment with the work of the principal on behalf of the school. It seemed to me that these interactions with staff were quite natural and could be part of everyday conversations.

I recall a lesson learned well with Allan, my very first principal. I was sitting with Allan in the staff common room when the head of boarding descended on me. She was unhappy about the behaviour of visiting schools who came to our school for debating. Her complaint was that the visiting debating teams would make a lot of noise entering and leaving the teaching block, which co-housed the district debating competition and boarders' study.

In front of Allan, she scolded me for not keeping the debaters' behaviour in check the night before.

Allan's response was swift and decisive – "You could do better than admonish Paul, and do everything you can to support him and our debating programs. Have you asked Paul how you can support him?"

Talk about dragging a staff member into alignment with the values and beliefs of the school!

Debating and public speaking was a huge activity in our school, widely promoted as one of our best activities. Parents enrolled their children in our school because of the promise that we would develop the children's speaking and confidence.

I learned a very important lesson that day. All staff needed to work together seamlessly to support each other and align ourselves with the overall mission and vision of the school.

Uncompromising high expectations of staff

Often even the best and most experienced executive leaders are reluctant to step up to the plate, especially if it seems to be out of their lane. I liked to use this quote, attributed to Michelle Obama (Burdo, 2017).

If you are afraid to use your voice, give up your seat at the table.

I know the quote was directed to women who have board roles. I liked to use it for executive leaders who occupy a seat at the cabinet (or senior executive) table each week and offer nothing or very little to the strategic growth of the school. An executive leader who will come to the executive meeting each and every week and remain silent, offering no comment about agenda items, advancing nothing from their leadership portfolio in the school for others to think about, they are without a voice. I expected my executive leaders to lead, and would remind them that it was their responsibility. What we say, how we say it, when we say it, to whom we say it, and whether we say it in the proper context are critical components for tapping into our full leadership potential.

Another lesson I learned from Allan, when I was at Fairholme College, was that the level of staff commitment to the school's context really counted, and it was worth fighting for.

Allan would speak candidly to me about this part of his role and how developing his staff was vital to him realising his aspirations on behalf of the school. He knew that if he got this right, he could be successful in his mission for the school. Allan transformed the school from a quaint finishing school for wealthy families into one of Queensland's top five independent schools, matching the very best that the Brisbane schools could offer.

From these early experiences and lessons, I grew to have little or no tolerance for indifference or recalcitrance in staff.

Consistently across the case-study principals who were the subject of my research, if individual staff members were not progressing at the rate that the principal wanted, they would intervene and ensure that individual began progressing. Otherwise, the principal was not able to meet the expectations of the parents and the board.

There needs to be a hard edge to principals' expectations and accountabilities of their staff in independent schools.

I was prepared to work with staff, but at the end of the day, it would be my way. One of my colleagues said to me about her school, "The staff here know that I do not accept mediocrity. They know that if there is poor performance, it will be addressed, and they know I will move staff on if they aren't performing."

Staff in the case-study principals' schools were expected to accept and agree to the expectations that the principal was working to promote. It was not negotiable. They were expected to commit to the full value set of the school. Principals should be unyielding on this.

But how do you mitigate spending a lot of time recalibrating staff?

Well, you have to recruit, select and promote the right staff. This was my strategy for building and sustaining the culture I wanted in my schools. When you employ staff in your school, hold the unwavering expectation that they must submit to the school's objectives and direction. If they do not, don't keep them employed.

There is a mathematical concept called exponential growth. Simply put, an exponential rate of increase becomes quicker and quicker as the thing that increases becomes larger. It has application here – the longer you tolerate under-performance or non-compliance the more time and energy it consumes, like a black hole.

If a staff member is not committed to the school's direction, get involved early and act. And if you don't get the change you want, move them on. In my early career I felt I could change everybody if they weren't committed. I felt that everybody was salvageable, that you could recalibrate even the most ardent contrarians – later in my career I became less tolerant. My experience has taught me that it takes a lot of time, effort, energy and money to recalibrate staff; that is why my tolerance has lowered later in my career.

I had a case where the recruitment panel, with me on board, made a bad appointment with a new IT manager. The main problem was that the fellow was a poor fit, culturally and contextually. In the first month he was absent more times than he was present, and when he was present, he was "absent." As soon as I began the proper process to hold him accountable, he elicited the support of a willing, equally recalcitrant, HR manager. And then the grief started.

The panel was involved from the outset, from reviewing applications right up to the agreement to appoint. How did we get it so wrong? What are the early signs to look for that someone is not a good cultural fit?

First of all, evaluate how the interviewee interacts with panellists and with people outside of the interview, your EA, for example. Having an interviewee speak with multiple people is important to determining their cultural fit. Ask all staff who met the interviewee what they thought about fit.

Ask lots of open-ended questions so that the interviewee has to speak about themselves, who they are, what they value, what sort of a person they are. Ask "odd" interview questions that seem to have nothing to do with the job.

Consider whether they show an understanding of your workplace culture.

In the case above, I saw the warning signs, but others on the panel were focused on technical skills and the objective criteria we set for the desirable candidate.

Besides recruitment, the work you do to build staff alignment to the mission and purpose of the school, and the effort you make to get staff on board are good mitigating strategies. If you have a strongly aligned staff culture, then the new staff member will more easily assimilate via the culture that you have developed.

Judicious delegating

While it is important for a principal to hold their staff to account, it is also important to delegate core aspects of the school's operation to critical executive staff, and to the middle and senior leaders in your school. You can't do the lot, but you must stay tuned to what is going on, and who is making important decisions.

To do this, you must trust yourself, your judgement, and your instincts. And you have to put your faith in others who you know are trustworthy.

One of the first matters you will attend to when you are appointed to your new principalship will be to build a quality executive or senior leadership team around you. You will do this by purposefully selecting people who you know will be able to lead and manage the school successfully across the important operational areas. Don't tolerate an inept senior manager.

With a quality team around you, you can confidently delegate and distribute decision-making to the executive team and give autonomy to the staff who directly report to you. While giving general autonomy, do check in regularly with your team one-on-one and in team meetings. This will enable you to provide guidance and direction, to review progress being made and to recalibrate strategy if you feel this is necessary. Through these meetings, you can reinforce your own thinking and values and beliefs so that the team understands and supports your aspirations.

The case-study principals showed a willingness to embrace new initiatives and introduce innovative programs to address the needs of the students. These initiatives required the principal to work with their staff to ensure that the staff adopted and committed to such programs. This work is contextual and is different for each of the case-study principals. The benefit of this approach is that staff are empowered to contribute great ideas and approaches that you may not think of.

Teacher appraisal

Systemic, significant and sustained teacher appraisal processes lead to improved outcomes for all students in our schools (Goe, 2007). It is terribly important if you are to hold staff to account that you have robust, effective appraisal systems in place in your school. Not annual appraisals, per se, but a process of ongoing self-improvement and quality feedback at any point in time.

Quality educational outcomes is the most important consequence of a child's or young adult's experience in our schools. As principals, we know that teacher quality and quality learning are the most important factors that influence student achievement.

After forty years in schools, I know that effective teacher appraisal is a key lever for increasing the focus on quality teaching and learning.

In my view, there are seven key elements that must be contained in an effective performance appraisal system:

1. Teachers are involved in the process
2. Teacher and school leaders have a shared understanding about the process and what constitutes quality.
3. Teachers have opportunities to express their perceptions and concerns throughout the process.
4. Principal, school leaders and teachers have confidence in the process.

5. The process is ongoing, it is not a once-a-year event. It is about continuous dialogue, review, and feedback to move teaching practice forward.

6. The process must have a conclusion, a clear report provided to the teacher showing areas of strength, areas for development, check-in points to evaluate progress and an appropriate allocation of resources to support any development plan.

7. As the principal, you own the process. It is important that any appraisal process you have in place comes with your endorsement and that you maintain oversight of the processes, even if you are not directly involved.

Appraisal can be a positive opportunity to share and provide clarity on expectations, to recognise achievement and to put plans in place for development and improvement. This is good for staff morale and culture. Staff can feel heard, validated and gain clarity and perspectives where they might not have been so sure of what direction the school was taking.

A crucial component of appraisals is follow-through of the process outcomes and actions – hold people to account to see that agreed objectives and action items happen.

Principal appraisal

It is a challenge to recommend a one-size-fits-all approach to appraisal. The main stumbling block is that each school's context is so different, and so the leadership context is also different.

There are five elements of appraisals that ought to be present in quality appraisal processes for principals.

1. Keep in the mind the purpose. In my view, appraisal is for the growth and development of the principal, geared to support the principal's effectiveness in the role.

2. The process needs to be linked to the principal's position description and key accountabilities drawn from the contract. This means the process is a function of the expectations held for the principal.

3. The process must be mutually agreed between the board chair (employer) and the principal. Whatever form the appraisal takes,

it must be mutually agreed. There are lots of models that are easily accessed through organisations like AHISA and AITSL.

4. I do not recommend using external commercial firms or HR organisations for appraisal. It is a professional process, and the professional associations are best for this.

5. Just as for teachers, the process must have a conclusion and a clear development plan, provided by the chair to the principal.

What did I learn from many conflict situations?

As I reflect on the successful times, the following strategies seemed to work best for me.

1. Breathe, breathe, breathe. Then work out how to resolve the conflict. Take your time planning your management of the matter. Seek input/advice from your most trusted executive. Seek ongoing advice from your HR coach/consultant, or team member. You are seeking advice, not asking someone to run the show for you. And seek legal advice if it is appropriate for the context.

2. Address the issue privately. This allows all parties involved the chance to express their feelings and intentions in a safe environment and prevents bystanders from getting needlessly involved. Spend some time with the protagonists understanding the issues and concerns. Get the full context. This can be time consuming and draining, but it is time well spent in the early stages of managing the conflict for a successful outcome.

3. Determine the most appropriate approach to deal with the issue. Deciding whether this should be done within the office – typically the best choice, especially in work-related matters – or outside of the office – over lunch, coffee or a walk – is also important. Regardless, it's important to make sure the approach chosen is appropriate for the issue and people involved. Don't use emails to try and resolve the conflict. Always use face-to-face meetings with factual notes taken of the meeting outcomes. I have found this to be useful to refer to, especially if needing to write a report later down the track.

4. Create an opening for communication so that everyone can have their say. Once an approach is decided on to address the conflict, give the individual or everyone involved a chance to have their say. Frame the conversation by stating that a conflict occurred and reinforcing the fact that everyone should have a chance to express their understanding and feelings about the situation – and then allow each person to have that chance.

5. Step back and let them have their say individually, with no interruptions, outbursts or judgment. Allowing everyone to be heard can often clear the air right from the start – and then you can dive into the actual issue itself. Have a set of guidelines or parameters, such as remaining respectful.

6. Use active listening techniques when addressing the conflict. Giving feedback as you listen, using small encouragements to show you're listening, and restating the issues – as well as pausing between statements – can be powerful ways to let someone else know you're listening and engaged.

7. Repeat back your understanding of the issues. While this is one of the major features of active listening, it deserves a callout of its own. As principals, we all perceive things differently and, unfortunately, our communication methods haven't evolved to beaming our thoughts into each other's heads at will. Taking every step to avoid a misunderstanding is important, especially in conflict resolution. By restating your understanding of the issues or conflict back to the individual you're speaking with, you solidify your own understanding and give the other person in the conversation a chance to correct you if you've misinterpreted their words.

8. Lean into the silence in difficult conversations. Our instinct can be to fill the silence when there's a gap in the conversation, especially if that silence is awkward or difficult. In conflict resolution, that silence is very different. Dig into those silences when having a difficult conversation so that the others involved have a chance to reflect and consider their responses. Allow time for everyone to carefully consider questions or start statements that can be difficult

for them. Encourage thoughtfulness, and don't feel the need to fill in silences when dealing with a topic that doesn't necessarily have an easy answer. It is ok not to have an answer. You can always say you need to reflect or sleep on it. Silence is golden.

9. Understand when it's out of your hands. Regardless of our efforts and conflict resolution prowess, there might be situations where there is no resolution that a principal can bring to the table. If a situation is too messy or difficult to resolve on your level, it's time to realise it should be brought to the next step. Sometimes there is nothing you can do, so know when to escalate.

10. Follow up with a close-out conversation, email or call. It's nice to close out conflict resolution with a private follow up conversation in whatever manner is most appropriate. Restate the resolution that was come to, thank the individual for their involvement and communication in resolving things, and offer to be on hand for any future issues, thoughts or conversations they might want to have in the future. This helps make sure everyone is accepting of the place you've come to, and to know that the conflict has passed.

In hindsight

While I led the learning in my schools, I also made sure that my staff knew what was involved in being a large, complex organisation. Clarity and transparency were my tools. I worked hard to articulate my intents and purposes when it came to norms, expectations, and how prepared I was to hold people to account if staff chose not to be compliant.

The most important component in accountability is fluid, ongoing feedback through ethical conversations as soon as there is an issue. Don't wait for some system or cycle, or a formal feedback loop; act when you have the information. How you act becomes critical if your management of the process is to be effective.

If I had my time over again, I would have done more HR training – especially in the areas of conflict management, mediation and dispute resolution. I would have found a top shelf coach in this area. I know this will be against the grain in many schools now, and not to disparage the general profession of HR, but I would not delegate staff conflict issues to an HR employee. Staff conflict can cause you and your school so much grief, you need to make sure it is a responsibility you keep inside your portfolio. Elicit the counsel of a top-quality executive coach skilled and trained in media and conflict resolution.

Chapter 6

LEAD!

CULTURE

What is culture?

When I mention culture, I am referring to organisational culture. Organisational culture (Schein, 2004) is the way things are done in a school: a shared sense of purpose and vision; social behaviours and the way people interact with each other; norms, espoused values, beliefs, and assumptions; rituals, ceremonies and traditions; history and stories; people and relationships; architecture, symbols, and artefacts; and identity and image.

I have found that principals have strong views about the sort of organisational culture required if their schools are to successfully achieve their goals and aspirations. They have values and beliefs, and definite views about what needs to be done and how to get it done. Effective principals can articulate their intents and purposes when it comes to norms, expectations, and how they are prepared to hold people to account if staff choose not to be compliant.

Know this up front, your job is to set the culture in your school. Your community will expect that of you. They want you to establish the feel and tone they experience when they walk into your school.

Know also that you will be judged by it. You will be judged by the state of the grounds and how students wear their uniform. You will be judged by how often you appear at the "gates" each morning, greeting parents and children.

I know many a head of primary that runs the drop off every morning. The head of primary in one of my schools wore it like a badge and the parents loved him for it. You need to be upbeat and positively influence others to ensure a positive school culture. If the culture is not what you want, or what is desirable, fix it.

It is hard work, relentless, and you may not see the fruits of your labour for three to five years. You will encounter naysayers, critics and pessimists. They will tell you how it can't be done. Ignore them.

Take Gandhi's advice:

> *I will not let anyone walk through my mind with their dirty feet.*

During a case-study interview, one principal said, "The tone of the school gives a really good indication of how things are going and, in turn, if the head is doing a good job."

You will be judged by your school's culture

For all of you who have tried, and been criticised, or couldn't take the step to try something new, or just wanted to have a say and felt fear-gripped, this quote from Theodore Roosevelt is for you:

> *It is not the critic who counts; not the man who points out how the strong man stumbles, or where the doer of deeds could have done them better. The credit belongs to the man who is actually in the arena, whose face is marred by dust and sweat and blood; who strives valiantly; who errs, who comes short again and again, because there is no effort without error and shortcoming; but who does actually strive to do the deeds; who knows great enthusiasms, the great devotions; who spends himself in a worthy cause; who at the best knows in the end the triumph of high achievement, and who at the worst, if he fails, at least fails while daring greatly, so that his place shall never be with those cold and timid souls who neither know victory nor defeat. (Evers, 2013, p 287)*

The president may have been referring to the stick he was copping from his democratic counterparts, but this is nonetheless one of my favourite quotes. It highlights a fundamental leadership paradigm. It taught me that when trying to improve a situation in my school or to achieve important change, I would often be confronted by critics. Typically phrases such as "nothing ever changes" and "that won't work around here" would be thrown around. In these situations, I drew on the words from Theodore Roosevelt. I have learned that the only thing that truly never changes is the presence of a critic for every moment of progress. Ignore them!

The criteria for judging the effectiveness of an independent school principal should concentrate on the school culture. As one of the case-study principals said:

> If I was judging effectiveness … I'd want to find out what the school tone and culture and that sort of thing is. I've advised boards when they are choosing a head, go spend a day with the applicant in their school. Get a feel for them in their school. Go see them on assembly. See them walk around, see how they interact with staff and students. You've got to walk in and observe and get a feel and a tone.

I say the same to parents who are choosing a school for their child. Go to the school when it is in session, not after hours. Go when there are kids in the playground, when they are interacting with fellow students and with teachers. Observe and note what you see. Do the students acknowledge you and greet you? How do they make you feel? This does not happen by chance, this is a direct result of the principal's leadership, modelling, example and expectations.

I used this to my advantage in one of my schools. Our main competitor was an easy 30-minute drive from us, and a bus serviced both schools. I would say to parents – make a visit during the school day and observe the climate, the tone and atmosphere, the presentation of the grounds, and so on. Our competitor was tucked away in the inner CBD of a large city, with no playing fields to speak of and students in congested spaces. I would trump the other school most times.

Culture is manifested in many ways, how the grounds are looked after is one. The tone, the feel is another – are there students pushing and shoving, do you get a sense that there is aggression? In all schools, you can quickly find out where the troublemakers are sitting. How do they treat you when you start talking to them? Are they dismissive? A visitor comes – does the student just grunt and point or is the student courteous, taking them to the place they want to go?

I felt throughout my leadership terms that I wanted each school to be better than what it was. This isn't an absolute term, but a relative one. I felt I owed it to my students and staff to be the best we could be, and that the best was a constantly moving target, like the horizon. You never reach the horizon.

Changing culture

The importance of fostering a great school culture can't be overemphasised. If you fail to place high importance on internal school culture, or if you allow a toxic culture to grow and spread, you are bound to experience endless difficulties, from sleepless nights and anxious board meetings to challenges to your leadership.

It is important as a new principal that you spend time evaluating the culture that exists. It is important to align with the ethos and foundations of the school in an authentic way, and not to simply adopt the existing culture without evaluating its appropriateness.

You must have the capacity to evaluate the existing culture against the fundamental beliefs and philosophy upon which the school is founded, and against your own values and beliefs. For me, if changes needed to be made, then it was my responsibility to plot a strategic course of action and engage the community in the process of realising the change.

A colleague of mine who is a CEO in the not-for-profit arts sector told me that she addressed a toxic culture in her workplace by attending to its physical layout. A terrible, dark layout – where staff gathered in each other's offices out of sight of the CEO – contributed to an undesirable culture. The CEO moved the whole workplace and redesigned the layout to open plan. The office was tastefully decorated to offer a pleasant atmosphere. Resistant staff left and what remained was a collegial, open and friendly workplace culture. It took some effort, but according to my colleague, it was well worth it.

At the focus group discussions as part of my research, the views of the group were reflected in this comment from one of the case-study principals:

It was the deliberate adjustment of culture that was a significant responsibility of the principal. If, in the view of the principal, the culture is not right, then it is their job to adjust it.

The case-study principals agreed that if the culture is not what they wanted, then they would work at addressing this; and they agreed this is a significant part of their role.

A principal mate of mine had this beautiful saying – "I tell staff, if they don't like change, don't look in the mirror."

Whatever age your school is, say forty years, it is your job to make sure it is still here in another forty years. As principals, we are custodians, we have the responsibility to sustain the vision of our forebears and to hold dear their traditions, values, ethos and culture. And we also have the responsibility to embrace change. I used to quote Socrates to my executive:

"Focus your energy not on fighting the old, but on building the new."

Culture is like the wind. It is invisible, yet its effect can be seen and felt. When it is blowing in your direction it makes for smooth sailing. When it is blowing against you, everything is more difficult.

For schools seeking to become more adaptive and innovative, culture change is often the most challenging part of the transformation. But culture change can't be achieved through top-down mandate. It lives in the collective hearts and habits of people and their shared perception of "how things are done around here."

As the principal of a school, I was in a position of authority – delegated authority from my board and community. I could mandate changes if I wanted to – and at times I did. I was judicious in what changes I would mandate. Show people the change you want to see. Let them feel part of it.

I arrived at a school where hats were compulsory all year around. Yet this was poorly managed – there was a lacklustre approach to insisting hates were worn, and inconsistent consequences were being applied for non-compliance. I observed the goings on for a couple of years, watched teachers fighting with kids to get them to do the right thing, and watched kids carrying their hats like a handbag – it was demoralising. So, I decided I would take a far more pragmatic approach. As a school in NSW with cold-cool temperatures throughout the winter months and low UV factor, I decided hats would be worn only in the summer months of term 1 and term 4. Kids were far more agreeable to this, and I had a good argument why it should be this way – so I mandated it. Compliance was still a struggle, but it became a whole lot better than it had been. What is the lesson here? Sometimes you just have to make the call, without collaboration or consultation – that's your job.

When did I collaborate? I wanted to change the wellbeing structure in another school from a vertical house system to a horizontal year group system, where the year level mentor groups would journey together from year 7 to year 12 with the same mentor. This involved a whole system of wellbeing, academic and pastoral support around the child. This was a significant cultural change, which took me nearly two years of meetings and informal talk, lots of conversations helping key staff understand the concept, and working together as a team to bring the idea to reality. In the end, I achieved what I wanted, but the heads of house said it was their idea. Perfect!

When it came to culture, I knew I had to make changes sparingly and at a snail's pace. I have seen principals overuse their authority in the hopes of accelerating transformation, and it rarely ends well. One of the most exasperating, career-ending scenarios for principals is this one.

The board employs the new principal with a clear mandate to clean out the dead wood, shake up the staff, get the right people on the bus, and all of those cliches that mean achieve a clean out. The board, at the point they offer the contract, convince the new principal they have the authority and backing to do the job.

The enthusiastic principal gets stuck into the task. This is how it unfolds in so many schools:

1. The principal starts the clean out
2. A few feathers get ruffled, the troops get restless
3. Some executive leaders are in the principal's sights
4. A nerve is struck
5. One executive leader with significant influence, usually at board level, rallies the troops
6. On occasion a petition is signed (it usually doesn't work)
7. The disgruntled staff get a hearing with a director or two or, more fatally, with the chair

8. The board decides that the principal has stepped outside the mandate and has gone rogue
9. The board starts applying the pressure on the principal
10. An external consultant is engaged to evaluate the situation and the brief given is to find against the principal
11. The principal is terminated.

On the other hand, I have seen principals shy away from organisational friction. Harmony is generally a preferred state, after all. And the success of an organisational transition is often judged by its seamlessness. In any change, a moderate amount of friction is okay. A complete absence of friction probably means that very little is actually changing. Look for the places where the action faces resistance and experiences friction. These often indicate where the dominant organisational design and culture may need to evolve. And where you will need to apply your elbow grease.

And remember that culture change only happens when people act. So, start there. While articulating a mission and changing school structures are important, it's often a more successful approach to tackle those sorts of issues after you've been able to show people the change you want to see.

At one of my schools, I was frustrated that there were very few community service opportunities for our students. They were mainly one-off events, such as taking a group of students to the local wetlands to clean up rubbish. I wanted to see sustained service opportunities that were continual and part of our annual co-curricular programs. I shared activities and opportunities with the wellbeing team, but they didn't take them up. I felt they didn't want to make a commitment to a long-term project, instead supporting single day, one-off activities.

In response, I set about forming a service club, which took a lot of time and effort. I noticed that once the group was established and doing effective work in the school and wider communities, including internationally, the mindset of the wellbeing team changed as they embraced more sustaining programs, which longer term changed the school's culture.

Watch for a toxic school culture. I know the cost of a toxic school culture: harassment, bullying, employee rights violations, and other abuses flow from a toxic environment.

Toxic culture takes an emotional toll on staff. At the end of the day, staff in these cultures go home to families drained, exhausted and negative. Good employees will leave, dragged down by under-performers. They will seek out a more positive culture.

Staff will call in sick when they don't feel like going to work because of a negative workplace culture. The stress of a toxic workplace takes a toll on employee health and increases the school's costs due to medical leave that staff take.

If a staff member is seriously affected by the behaviour of another to such an extent that they are forced to resign it could cost you, as the employer, tens of thousands of dollars in legal costs and settlement costs.

Context matters

One finding from my research was that:

> *Principal effectiveness hinges on the principal understanding and knowing their context: the leadership context from which they enact leadership, the organisational context, and the Australian independent school context. To lead effectively, principals must understand their organisation's context, appreciate how that context impacts on how they enact their leadership, and they must respond accordingly to the organisation's unique challenges and situations. (Teys, 2021)*

The parallels with CEOs of not-for-profit companies can clearly be seen. Context in this book includes such elements as organisational values and cultures, social and professional relationships and interactions, and the ways the principal/CEO is impacted, motivated, and even limited by local, national and international influences. It refers to the principal's surroundings, the people they work with and for, the challenges they must meet and accept, and the viability and sustainability of their school. School/organisational context impacts on how principal leadership is enacted in schools and mastery of context is crucial to a principal's effectiveness.

When I visited the four principals in each of their schools, I could feel, see and sense the culture.

Staff were relaxed in each other's company and the students were laid-back and comfortable chatting to teachers. Within the relaxed environment it was obvious that there was professional respect between teachers with the consideration they showed others and students showed respect for teachers by the greetings they used. I observed the free exchange of ideas in teams, and noted how team members did not appear to be inhibited in any way. I noticed that people didn't just walk past each other, there were greetings and acknowledgements, warm smiles. The grounds were immaculately kept and I noticed students picking up their rubbish as they moved off after break.

The climate that existed was a window into the culture. But it was different in each school, because of the school's context. For example, there are visible and nuanced differences between an Anglican church school of 1600 students in western Ipswich in Queensland and an Anglican church school of 1600 students in western Sydney in NSW, even though on the surface you might expect them to be similar.

I want to avoid stereotypes but, in my travels, I see country kids playing outside a lot more at lunch, using their school grounds and facilities. They are not hanging around the corridors and locker areas. The topic of their break chatter is different, the interests and concerns of a country kid are different to their city cousins.

Some differences are due to the concentrated population in the city, which creates a different social environment. City schools are generally more crowded and busier, the regional schools appear to be calmer and more peaceful.

At one school I could not help but sense I was in a great school; the tone, culture, and atmosphere were inspiring and uplifting. The principal blocked out the first 30 minutes in his day, from 8:00am to 8:30am, to meet and greet staff and students (parents were restricted to drop off zones only, outside the school). The principal made sure he made eye contact, engaged, and sustained a conversation for a minute or longer. Wind forward a couple of hours in my day when I was walking around the school on my own. The students greeted me and engaged with me in a natural way. The leadership provided by my colleague was evident for me to see.

The case study principals explained how they would select their executive leaders, and other employees, who they believed would support their school's context, culture and the direction that they had for the school.

Those who build great organisations make sure they have the right people on the bus and the right people in the key seats before they figure out where to drive the bus. They always think first about who and then about what. When facing chaos and uncertainty, and you cannot possibly predict what's coming around the corner, your best "strategy" is to have a busload of people who can adapt to and perform brilliantly no matter what comes next. Great vision without great people is irrelevant. (Collins, 2001)

When change was not going to plan, I would use my authority to insist on new behaviours that would produce the outcome that I wanted. As the CEO, I would insist on certain non-negotiable behaviours and targets, and I would expect them to be met. I was prepared to act to address issues early; I wouldn't shy away from it, as hard as it could be emotionally and psychologically. Quite often the staff member in question would leave because they didn't like the parameters set for them.

I knew that I had to be aware of the contextual factors that were present in my schools because they influenced my behaviours and practices. I knew I had to be flexible and adaptable to my local school environment. I couldn't ignore the contextual factors, if I did, it would jeopardise my chances of achieving the goals and aspirations I had.

Plan the desired organisational culture

Changing organisational culture can seem like a trudge up an enormous hill with seemingly no end, especially when you're not sure where to begin. Most principals try to figure out exactly how to change school culture in a meaningful, lasting way, but struggle to come up with a clear method that is sustainable in the long term. To help with this, I have put together a ten-point plan, which I found worked for me.

1. Start by making sure there's a clear rationale for why the culture should change
2. Examine your mission, vision and values for both the strategic and the value-based components of the organisation. Your management team needs to answer questions such as:
   a. What are the five most important values you would like to see represented in your organisational culture?

b. Are these values compatible with your current organisational culture? Do they exist now? If not, why not? If they are so important, why aren't you attaining these values now?

c. Are your mission, vision and values clearly articulated and disseminated so that employees have a clear understanding of the organisation's direction and where they and their goals fit within it?

d. What cultural elements support the success of your organisation, and what elements of the current organisational culture need to change?

3. Develop a picture of your school's desired future, short term and out to twenty years

4. Clearly define the non-negotiables. When contemplating a culture change, look at your current culture and call out the aspects you want to retain. Which are up for negotiation?

5. What sort of school do you want to be for the key stakeholders?

6. How will this benefit your employees and the organisation's other stakeholders?

7. Don't rush it. Changing a culture can take anywhere from months to several years. It doesn't happen overnight. It really depends on accessing the true gap between the culture you have and the culture you need to have.

8. Deal with the low-hanging fruit relatively quickly. This may mean dealing with toxic staff or addressing complaints that are easy to fix.

9. Invest now. Don't wait for staff and resources that may never come. It takes years of investment to get to a point where your culture becomes part of how you behave and act, so begin whatever way you can.

10. Be bold and lead.

In hindsight

Designing the culture you want requires an intentional plan. A positive, accountable and empowering culture doesn't just happen. Start by identifying where you are today. Then, identify what kind of culture you and your team want in your school. Compare the two lists. If there is a gap between the culture you have and the culture you want, create a vision for change. Develop an intentional plan to shift the behaviours and attitudes to align with your desired culture.

My experience has taught me that organisational culture is a complex web of relationships. As those relationships change and shift over time, work must be put in by you, the executive, employees, and management alike to maintain positive change and continue along a productive path.

I and many colleagues have successfully achieved cultural change in ways that created long-lasting improvements for our school communities. When challenges loom, damaging your hard work, my best advice is to reach out to colleagues who have achieved sustained change. They will be a font of wisdom and so keen to support you. Avoid engaging a consultant that has had no experience or success in changing culture in a school. This contextual experience is so terribly important.

Like all relationships, the foundation of true change to organisational culture starts with trust. So, first of all, establish the school's trust and confidence in you as the principal.

OPEN-DOOR POLICY?

You must decide early what your stance on an open-door policy will be. How accessible do you want to be?

I knew from the start that I wanted to be visible, accessible and available, yet this priority competed with the sheer workload I had. There was a real temptation to close the door and bury myself in my work.

As friendly and inviting as I tried to be, and thought I was, the title of principal carries a lot of weight and can create an atmosphere of intimidation. I knew that. The title alone can dissuade your staff from approaching you to chat about matters that are important to them, and by extension to the school's performance.

To combat this, I tried to create an atmosphere of approachability, I encouraged staff to share ideas, concerns and feedback that were important to them, and to be frank about what they felt was important to the school's success.

To achieve that atmosphere, I had an open-door policy. By this I mean more than having your door physically open; it is a metaphor for the way I wanted to operate – people could approach me to discuss any matters of interest or concern to them.

I know of a principal who writes a birthday card to every student and hand-delivers it on their special day, as part of the priority he places on positive relationship-building and regard for students. His school in Sydney's north has close to 2400 students.

After my first principalship – which was a very positive experience – I knew how important it was for a me to work hard at personal relationships to foster trust and confidence and to build a culture where staff could be candid with me. I knew that my influence could not be based on my position but on my credibility and staff's trust in me as the leader.

The parents in schools that I have led expected that I would be available and accessible to them. So did staff, past students, board directors and so on. That is the expectation in fee-paying independent schools.

The dilemma for many principals is how to make yourself available, accessible and approachable to your community. Is this even desirable? How do you resolve the tension between managing workload and spending important time with people? Is accessibility and availability a veneer?

I remember the principal that preceded me at one of my schools had a notorious open-door policy. His EA would say,

> *"He's fond of saying his door is always open, but he's seldom ever there."*

The benefits of an open-door policy

There are five obvious benefits that come to mind for me. An open-door policy:

1. Demonstrates to others that you are accessible as the boss
2. Sends messages to staff that you value an open flow of communication
3. Allows your staff to gain fast access to important or unfolding situations or information

4. Really serves you well to maintain closer working relationships with your staff
5. Gives you the opportunity to say hello to people who are outside your office for other reasons.

I found that if I had high levels of accessibility, it was far more likely staff would feel comfortable stopping by for a quick chat to bring difficult issues, situations or ideas to my attention. I would also call out if I saw a staff member outside – purposefully saying hello. They would then stick their head in for a chat. This then extended to when I was in the grounds – staff were happy to engage with me. Particularly when I was lining up for a coffee at the cafeteria – they knew that if they timed it right, I would shout coffee. We got a lot solved "on the run." As an open-door principal, I had a much better understanding and "pulse" on what was happening in the school than if I had hidden under a rock like a hermit crab.

I also found that my open-door approach gave me easier access to more informal discussions – and these are the discussions that often lead to important insights about the school. I know my colleagues who would shut their doors a lot found that they were not in the loop with what was happening in the school. A closed-door policy, without trying to polarise this, can send the unintentional message that you are uninterested in and disengaged from daily activities.

My open door was symbolic of how I liked to operate more broadly. It enabled closer working relationships, promoted a culture of friendly openness and built a belief in others that I wanted to be actively engaged with the daily life of the school. A closed door can generate a feeling of formality in the work environment, as well as a feeling of secretiveness, which can negatively affect relationships with subordinates.

When a principal's door is often closed, over time it can create a barrier between them and their executive and senior teams. This barrier can negatively affect many aspects of work, from creating an environment where employees are afraid to speak freely, to building a belief in others that you are disengaged from the school's operations or just not interested. It may even cause your executive team to feel that you are not trusting of them or that you withhold important information.

Don't lock yourself away. Opening your office and your workspace allows you to be a strong pillar of support for your staff and students. Healthy interactions amongst the employees are essential for a positive ambience in the workplace, you can set the example for this.

All of what I have said above equally applies to relationships with students.

Five years ago a student named George began regularly popping up to my office to say hello. He would pop in to talk rugby league, as we were both mad Queensland supporters. Through our footy chats I became a mentor to him. I know he will be sending me messages the evening before the NRL grand final between his beloved Rabbitohs and the Panthers. He also knows he can contact me when he is on a downer.

Overcoming problems caused by an open-door approach

One oft-cited objection to an open-door approach is that you can become everyone's sounding board or problem solver.

I know that my open-door policy created some tensions with my executive and senior teams when staff brought concerns to me, seemingly over the head of their line manager. I concede that this can create frustration and waste time among executive and senior managers. But in my view, the benefits outweigh the perceived issues.

On the other hand, there are staff who believe they need to go as high as possible for the resolution of even the simplest issues. I found that this was easily overcome by closing any such situation with, "I will be happy to provide in-principle support but you will need to speak to [appropriate leader/manager]."

Sometimes, I saw this approach result in staff bringing up problems they could have resolved on their own, which can be tedious for those tasked with looking into things. I didn't see that as an issue – the long-term benefit of a staff member feeling valued and being heard was worth it.

If too many staff go over the head of their supervisor, it can eliminate that component of the supervisor's role and lessen his or her influence. I found that was easily mitigated by giving the supervisor a quick briefing about the casual meeting and the outcome. You do need social and interpersonal skills to make this work, some principals are more receptive than others to listening to staff concerns – this can create a situation in which some principals are bombarded with issues while others are not. Consider your own skills and preferences before deciding to invite this into your role.

There are times when principals, even with an open-door policy, must shut their door. One such occasion is during confidential employee discussions. My advice is that, unless you are engaged in sensitive, highly confidential business, keep your door open. When my door was closed, people knew it was for good reason.

School and corporate culture are changing rapidly. Many colleagues have adopted the open-door culture for all its benefits, which far outweigh the drawbacks. I wanted more transparency at all levels in the school and felt this was the best way to set the example and build the culture.

How to manage workload with an open-door policy

An open-door policy might seem like your door is literally always open, but it doesn't have to mean that you are constantly interruptible. Constant interruption prevents you from thinking deeply and serving your school in the ways only you can. To do your best, you need thinking time, quiet time and sometimes longer periods of uninterrupted time. If you allow too many unscheduled intrusions into your day, you won't be able to lead.

The best advice I can give is to block out a set amount of time in your diary for deep thinking, say 90 minutes in the morning and again in the afternoon, where your EA knows you are not to be interrupted. This technique is called "time blocking" (Doist, 2021). Time blocking, or calendar blocking, involves defining specific time blocks for the tasks, events, and activities in your life, and then scheduling them against your calendar.

Time blocking

For further reading on time blocking and how it might help you:

- https://todoist.com/productivity-methods/time-blocking
- https://www.projectmanager.com/blog/time-blocking-guide
- https://www.ntaskmanager.com/blog/time-blocking/
- https://biz30.timedoctor.com/time-blocking/

How can you give yourself place, time and space to focus while maintaining an open-door culture? These six practices have worked for me.

1. *Scheduled open-door times*

   There will be times that you are busy and times that you may have a bit more breathing room in your schedule. If you still want to give your team the opportunity to come and speak with you, offer them specific times during the day when you expect to be less busy than others.

   This availability may change but do your best to keep them aware of when you are free to assist them throughout the day. You can either let them schedule small increments of time with you, or simply allow them to come in on a first come, first served basis.

2. *Have weekly one-on-one meetings*

   A great way to check in with key reports is by having weekly or fortnightly one-on-ones. Depending on the size of your team, these may be less frequent to allow each member the opportunity to share their current workload and address any questions for you.

   Schedule these for the same day and time each week, so you both know when to be prepared for the conversation. These visits can prevent much of the need for additional chats throughout the rest of the week.

   Prepare discussion points – jot down a list of bullet points that you'd like to discuss. Ask your direct report to do the same.

3. *Schedule team meetings*

   Block regular time in your schedules – it doesn't necessarily matter how often they occur, but it is important that you schedule them on your calendar as a repeating event.

   Just as team members need to meet with their manager, they often need to meet with one another as well. Holding a team meeting at least once a month will give you an opportunity to meet with the full team and review goals, projects and upcoming milestones. Depending on your collaborative and consultative approaches, you might need to hold them more frequently.

   These meetings should always have a firm purpose, along with a prearranged agenda of topics to go over. This will avoid any unnecessary details sneaking into the conversation.

4. *Have ground rules and standards*

   While you should have a desire to connect with your team on a personal level, it is important that you and your team recognise the professional relationship above all. If you have an open-door policy, a standard must be set that these times are to discuss professional, business-related manners. They can be friendly and jovial of course, but the main purpose should be business.

5. *Use the communication apps that are available*

   A great feature of an open-door policy is the ability for the executive and others to communicate with you in more ways than simply face-to-face. Online tools like Toggl Plan make it possible for employees to feel empowered to make their own decisions and self-manage their tasks. As questions arise, integrated tools like Slack are available to send queries to the manager about current projects. Agile and Asana are good software programs for managing projects.

6. *Use your phone*

   Early in my career I was dead set against using my mobile phone for work. My first mobile was a Nokia 2110. That gives my age away!

   I felt the mobile was for personal use, and any use of it in my work would be construed as "off task." I have changed my view. My iPhone can save me a lot of time and energy in my day. It is a handsome personal organiser; using messages is a powerful time saver. Learn to use your mobile to save you time and effort.

In hindsight

I found that an open-door policy worked really well for me because it sent a clear, visible message to all my staff that my door was open to every employee, parent and student. Subliminally, I was also sending a message that I could see what's going on and I was part of it. I wanted to encourage open communication, feedback and discussion about any matter of importance to my staff, students or parents. I wanted my community to bring their concerns, questions or suggestions to me and I was comfortable with it being outside of the usual "chain of command."

I had an open-door policy to develop trust and to make sure important information reached leaders who could use it to make improvements.

COMMUNICATE, COMMUNICATE, COMMUNICATE

Principals must work tirelessly on effective communication and community relations. When you communicate effectively you inspire optimism and hope in others. Part of your role is to set the tone and climate in your school. Your community feeds off you. Highly effective principals employ well-crafted, effective communications to ensure that all in their community are engaged and supportive. You are the storyteller!

Over many years and for various reasons I have reviewed the prospectuses for principal appointments, and two traits or skills appeared consistently in every single one: interpersonal and communication skills. Boards expected expertly honed communication skills.

Effective communication builds understanding and trust. When teachers and parents or carers understand and trust you as the principal, your school is better able to work with the whole community to support children's wellbeing and development. Effective communication is the key to establishing and maintaining positive partnerships with parents and carers.

During the peak of COVID-19 transmissions, when political leaders were making daily announcements that impacted our school's operations, I would send a daily 3pm email to parents. Replies to this email allowed me to keep my finger on the pulse of parent opinion and I was able to use the feedback to bolster or validate decisions.

Face-to-face communication

Late in my career, as I reflect on parent partnerships and the relationships with parents, I am now inclined to pick up the phone or arrange a face-to-face meeting, rather than manage communications through emails, letters or newsletters. I have found face-to-face meetings to be most effective.

One of the great joys in working in P–12 schools is the beautiful exchanges you have with little children. It is an art, being able to communicate effectively with a six year old. There is an old show-business adage – never work with children or animals. I don't know about the animals, but although children can behave unpredictably most are adorable.

My supervising practice teacher at Kenmore South Public School told me, when communicating face-to-face with a child, to "connect before you direct." He suggested squatting to the child's eye level before talking.

I recall a morning greeting with two kindy kids who were walking down the path, seemingly full of business and knowing exactly what they were meant to be doing. They stopped to chat to me. I squatted to their eye level, greeted them using their names, and kept it simple (as I had been taught to do). "What do you have on this morning?" I asked them.

The boy replied, "My shirt, tie and my blazer."

Tips for effective face-to-face communication with parents

Always listen carefully. Try not to interrupt – think about how much you would dislike it yourself. Appreciate critics and thank them. Treat each conversation as crucial.

Ensure you stick to the purpose of the meeting; take advantage of face-to-face meetings to initiate new discussion about things of importance to you and your school. Make notes. In particular, record agreed times and dates. Put follow-up actions in your calendar.

Work on reducing your use of conversation dead-air fillers like "um" and "er", as well as cliches and phrases such as "you know", "basically", "to be honest", "at the end of the day", "the fact of the matter is", "sort of thing", and so on.

Difficult conversations with adults will occur. Don't become defensive – breathe and count to ten before you respond.

When speaking with parents, show that you are actively listening. I would repeat back to parents the main points that they were making to me, to show I was listening and taking on board their concerns. I would say (with sincerity and intent) that I would look into it. I did, and I got back to the parent with the outcome, or action, or what will happen next.

Speeches

Elegant, articulate speeches are fine; sophisticated or clever graphics are fun; but in the end, effective communications is all about the impact it has on others. Your greatest impact will come from one-on-one interactions and take note – every interaction counts.

In my experience, if you want to be an effective public speaker, less is almost always more. Don't be one of those principals who doesn't know when to sit down. Staff and students like short, impactful speeches, so set the standard early. I've seen new principals using media and digital presentations, which is fine occasionally. I found that kids really appreciated my 5-minute speeches with three important takeaways, an anecdote, and a good quality joke. Humour is important, but if it isn't your thing, don't try it.

Effective public speaking is impactful. Something should change because of what you have to say. The children listening to you, or the parents or staff, should learn something new, or decide to do something differently or choose to embrace an aspirational goal because of what you said. Remember, you are the principal – everyone learns from you. Before you decide on the content of your communication, get clear about its intended outcome. What are you trying to achieve?

I always write things down when I am planning to communicate, not because I'm going to read it out loud, but because it helps me think and prepare myself. Are there words or phrases that are particularly helpful or especially confusing? What does my audience need to hear first, second, third? And what is the essence of this communication? In the second half of my principal career, I spoke without notes. It was very effective. The student leaders and aspiring student leaders would remark how impactful it was and they wanted to practice and get to the point where they could also manage it. Parent communication at a whole school level was far more impactful when I spoke without notes.

However, there are contexts when a well-rehearsed and intentionally delivered speech is required – it depends on the audience and the purpose.

When a more formal speech is called for that does require notes, I encourage people to write the speech up like an affidavit. Using a numbered notes system keeps each main point you want to make clearly separated in chronological order. This assists with eye contact and staying on track.

At speech day in 2003 I decided this was the way to go. I was 5 minutes from speaking to the Junior School assembly at Moreton Bay College. In my hand was my hard-bound folder, one speech inside, meticulously prepared. I looked at it, looked around at my audience of over a thousand people, and decided my speech was not going to cut it. I left it under my seat. I mentally decided three key takeaways, and the context, and went with it. It was lauded by the audience as one of the greatest speeches ever.

Nine key principles for effective communication

These key principles apply across schools and companies and are apt for principals and CEOs alike.

1. *Respect*
    Respect is the foundation of effective communication with parents, carers and families. Adopting a position of respect will help you as the principal better understand the parents, carers and families that you must work with. This includes respect for every family's:

    - Religious and cultural background, values, beliefs and languages
    - Parenting arrangements – blended families, co-parenting families, single-parent families and rainbow families, for example
    - Gender diversity – respect for parents and childrens gender and preferred pronouns, for example
    - Background – occupation, education and socio-economic features
    - Circumstances – parents with intellectual disabilities, same gender marriages, parents who are teenagers and families experiencing all manner of challenges.

2. *Listening*
    Listening is one of the most important keys to effective communication.

    When you listen well, you get more information about children and their families. You also get the full benefit of parents' and carers' in-depth knowledge of their children. And you show parents and carers that you value their experience, ideas and opinions and take their concerns seriously. You take the partnership with parents seriously.

I remember being in the middle of a rather intense (one-sided) conversation with a parent about how the netball coach had discriminated against her daughter in team selections. I went to speak and she made a very quick-witted remark, saying, "Oh, I'm sorry… did the middle of my sentence interrupt the beginning of yours?"

It completely diffused the tension as I couldn't help but break into laughter. That was just what we needed to get the conversation on an even keel.

Repeat back to the parent what they have been saying, in brief, to show that you have been listening to them.

3. *Speaking*

    In every interaction with parents and carers, one of your goals is to strengthen your partnership with them. You're more likely to achieve this goal if you consistently speak to parents in a clear and considerate way. Parents will respond well and connect with you in positive ways if you speak confidently, are authentic, use voice modulations to show you are engaged, show you have connected with affirming facial expressions, and demonstrate interest and comfort with your body language.

    Make sure you enunciate your words well. I recall an assembly at AB Paterson College when I was having a "rant" about the state of uniforms and how poorly I felt the students were wearing them, especially in public. I told the girls that I felt they looked tardy. This was returned to me via the parent of a student (who, I might add, wore her uniform immaculately) who told me, "I do take umbrage that you would refer to my daughter as a tart".

4. *Raise concerns early*

    As the principal, it is your job to surface concerns or issues early – don't sit on them. Build this into your school's culture, bring parents into a problem and invite them to be part of the solution as soon as a matter of concern emerges.

    I adopted a problem-solving approach and know now that it helped me work with parents to get good outcomes for problematic behaviours. Don't dwell on the child, or the problem, but work together to address concerns.

I used a simple six-step approach:

- Identify the problem
- Brainstorm as many solutions as possible
- Jointly evaluate the pros and cons
- Decide on a solution to try
- Put the solution into action
- Review the solution after a period.

One of the keys to this approach is talking about concerns when they come up. Problems usually don't go away by themselves. And if you let problems build up, they might be more and more difficult to address, usually resulting in a "dust up" with the parent and a breakdown in relationships.

5. *Respond with an ethic of care*

When parents and carers raise concerns with you, the basics of listening and speaking still apply. And respect and sensitivity are still key to effective communication.

Also, if you focus on the issue that parents are raising and remember that your shared goal is supporting their child, it can help you avoid defensiveness or justifications.

Sometimes the best way to help is simply listening to parents. Parents might just need to feel that their concerns have been heard. You don't always need to look for a solution straight away.

Day and Gurr (2014), in studying principals in Australian settings, found that an ethic of care was evident in all the highly effective principals they studied.

6. *Communicate often*

Make sure to communicate often! A common mistake amongst principals is simply not communicating enough, or only reaching out when there's a problem. Communicate regularly with parents and they won't be on high alert when they hear from you! This generation of parent, from gen Xers through to gen Yers (and especially the Yers) want to know what is going on, they are invested and want information. Don't let them down.

7. *Communicate in forms that work for parents and carers*

    One size does not fit all when it comes to parent-teacher communication. From apps, message boards and email, to social media, texting and phone calls, find out what communication tools work best for parents and carers, then stick with it. A simple survey can give you incredible insights into what parents want. Some available tools include:

    - https://www.surveymonkey.com/
    - https://www.questionpro.com/
    - https://surveysparrow.com/
    - https://www.surveylegend.com/

8. *Make parents feel valuable*

    Great parent-teacher communication starts with making parents feel valuable. All parents and carers have something worthwhile to offer your school, especially forming the triage partnership of child-school-parent. Parents can also support the school in other ways, helping at an event, speaking to students about their occupation, being part of a focus group to provide information to you as principal. They can support their children by attending school events, showing up for parent information evenings. Encourage parents to participate and share their strengths.

9. *Don't make assumptions*

    Don't blindly accept what somebody else tells you about the context or the circumstances of an event. Never make assumptions about a student's home life. Don't assume a student lives with two parents or any parent at all. Don't assume that English is a parent or guardian's native language. Be mindful of the fact that families come in all shapes, sizes and backgrounds. It is your job to know the families as well as the children.

    The worst mistake principals and leaders alike make when they first meet someone is to make assumptions about that person from the first contact.

Communications framework

What became important to me in my work, especially later in my career with the proliferation of emails, text message and social media commentary, was to develop a communications framework. A communications framework is your foundation for all internal and external messaging in your school and should align your school's values, goals, and objectives with behaviours that you want.

Frameworks of this kind are highly contextual. I would include rules and protocols for each of the following. I have included some examples that could be considered in your framework.

Social media – (individual) teachers should not be using social media for communicating with parents. Instead, emails (to protect teachers), phone calls, in-person meetings, and school approved software should be used.

Email – some parameters for professional email communications are:

- Do not reply to all; use bcc for class group emails
- Ensure that teachers are not sending emails outside school hours, especially on weekends. If they do, it can easily become the expected norm
- Use the 24-hour rule. If you receive a contentious or provoking email, wait 24 hours before replying
- Proof-read to be sure they are semi-formal, not casual – no matter how well a teacher knows a parent. Use salutations, date, and a short, meaningful subject
- Send an acknowledgement within 24 hours and a more detailed response within 72 hours
- Use a standard school signature.

Text messages – I recommend that teachers not use text messages to communicate with parents. To do so would mean that a parent has your mobile phone number, which is unwise, and the risk is excessive use and misuse.

Phone calls – use a school phone, not your mobile. Be polite and remain cheerful. Actively listen and take notes.

Face-to-face meetings – be on time, that means be early, don't keep parents waiting. Check before the meeting starts how much time they have and be respectful of that. Keep devices turned off. Use a note pad if you want to make notes.

It is important to develop your own values and beliefs around effective communication, and implement them in the context of your school.

Communication goes far beyond just talking

While speaking is one major component of communication, listening, writing, body language and other nonverbal cues are all equally important.

It's important to pay attention to your body language and tone of voice when you're having a conversation. Your mood, actions and demeanour can convey powerful messages.

Confidence in what you are saying and doing is essential. I have found that if I appeared confident, others were more likely to agree to what I might propose. Conversely, the less confident I appeared in delivering a message, the more objections I was likely to get.

Ensure the link between what you say and what you do remains close. Failure to follow through on a goal or promise will undermine your credibility. If a disparity develops between promise and action for any reason, explain why.

Remaining approachable while being regarded and consulted as a professional leader with significant knowledge about teaching and learning requires principals to maintain a cheerful demeanour, even if the going is tough. The grumpiness of a principal can quickly pervade their school.

School events

Treat all events as great communication opportunities. Make events as culturally reflective and responsible as possible. This means having an awareness and understanding of different cultures in your school and reflecting that at important celebrations and ceremonies. You can incorporate the customs and beliefs of the different cultures in your school in a way that is safe and supportive, not discriminatory or harmful. At one of my primary schools, we had a flag raised for each country that our children or their parents were originally from in an outdoor assembly space that was used regularly. A visual reminder of how important cultural understanding is.

At events, personally meet and greet as many parents and community members as possible. Try not to speak for too long. Keep the focus on student achievement and your school's current goals. Make it clear what the school's core business is.

Ensure students feel included and rewarded for their effort and achievement. Plan well for the P–12 assemblies and consider how you can be relevant to the whole audience.

Thank and acknowledge parents for their support in their children's learning and for the school.

At school presentation day ceremonies, I always made a commitment to speak to the children and to speak to the parents.

I loved to wrap up my end-of-year primary presentation day address with, "Have a great holiday with your children; this is the time of the year when parents come to love and appreciate the work that teachers do."

In hindsight

I learned that strong communication skills were the elixir to lasting influence and success. I worked tirelessly to see that these skills were consistently visible every day and in every interaction.

Remember that when you are a principal, or become one, you become a public figure and will be subject to much more scrutiny than you were as a teacher. Be clear, consistent and transparent so that all members of the community know that what they see is what they get. Enjoy answering questions and discussing the school vision and goals, and listen attentively to all community members.

SCHOOLS ARE COMPLEX SYSTEMS

Complicated systems have many moving parts, but they operate in patterned ways. Schools and people don't. For instance, flying a commercial aeroplane involves complicated but predictable steps, and as a result it's astonishingly safe. Schools are complex because they contain many interactive, interdependent and diverse elements.

Complexity in schools is a combination of the number of families and staff you have; the number of programs, services and activities you provide; the extent to which staff cooperate and engage in a variety of commitments outside of classroom teaching; the number of other schools and associations you operate in; and the number of people you employ.

Managed well, this kind of complexity helps rather than hinders your school's performance. However, some factors destroy value and productivity as well as adding complexity. These might include the amount of regulation in your school and how quickly it changes; the extent of duplication of effort, overlap of roles and responsibilities in your school; the frequency of change in your organisational structure; the rate of new staff appointments; and changes of strategy by competitor schools. This is the kind of complexity that you may well want to reduce.

The conductor metaphor is a good illustration of the systems thinking concept at work in principal leadership. Drucker (1988) claimed that leaders of large information-based businesses twenty years hence (circa 2008) would more likely resemble the conductor of a large symphony orchestra than the models of leadership in business.

> *There are probably few orchestra conductors who could coax even one note out of a French horn, let alone show the horn player how to do it. But the conductor can focus the horn player's skill and knowledge on the musician's joint performance. (Drucker, 1988, p 7)*

A modern full-scale symphony orchestra can have more than one hundred musicians, most often distributed across nine instrument sections; parallels with a school can easily be made.

Changes in complexity

Leading and managing an independent school today is fundamentally different than it was in 1999, when I accepted my first principalship. The most significant difference that I have come to know is in the level of complexity that principals have to manage. The complexities have been born out of such factors as the school's own determination to be competitive in the market, to offer outstanding educational programs for students, the bureaucratisation of independent schools by governments, the burgeoning industry of school compliance, and the increasing numbers of gen Y parents.

One complex situation arose when a former parent sought re-enrolment for her son. I had determined, after consultation with staff and parents of other children in the cohort, that a re-enrolment and return to the school would not be successful or beneficial. The student seeking re-enrolment had engaged in substantial bullying of other students. I had concerns for the safety and wellbeing of our own students should the re-enrolment be accepted.

In deciding to decline the enrolment, I made an appropriate decision based on the best interests of the broader student cohort and the duty of care and obligations I owed its students and their families.

Despite this, the parent made a complaint to the Human Rights Commission (HRC). I received a "please explain" letter from the Commissioner, with a veiled threat of being forced to attend a mediation session. The parent's complaint was that her child was not given priority to re-enrol.

I knew that in this case the HRC was on thin ice and there was no basis for discrimination, which are the grounds on which the HRC could act. I knew the HRC could not force me to take the enrolment. Nonetheless, I had to engage a human rights lawyer to fight the complaint, and put considerable time, effort and money into the matter. Not to mention that defending such decisions and being subjected to the accompanying scrutiny and criticism takes a toll psychologically.

There was no case for discrimination and the commissioner's assistant admitted this to me when we spoke on the phone about the matter. I learned that the commissioner could hear complaints about schools and if the parties are agreeable can act as a mediator. The parent asked the commission to close their complaint given I was unwilling to change my decision not to admit the child.

There have always been complex systems in schools, and schools have always been home to the unpredictable, the surprising, and the unexpected. Schools have always had to respond to the volatile world of league tables, PISA, NAPLAN, and a myriad of government-driven initiatives that should have no bearing on a child's learning and schooling.

But complexity has gone from something found mainly in large schools, such as inner-city schools, to almost all schools. Most of this increase has resulted from the information technology revolution of the past few decades. Systems that used to be separate are now interconnected and interdependent, which means that they are, by definition, more complex.

A few of the heavy hitters that were relatively unobtrusive in the 1990s but that I had to wrestle with every day in my principal life (in 2022) were:

- Complex human resources issues
- Compliance, legal and risk accountabilities
- Workplace health and safety
- The evolution of ubiquitous information technology systems
- The intrusion of social media into the veins of schools
- The avalanche of extra-curricular activities, clubs and societies
- Re-engineering curriculum, teaching and learning and pedagogy
- Emergence of highly specialised teams in schools, including:
  - Individual needs, student services and NDIS teams
  - Marketing, public relations, communications and events teams
  - Philanthropy, engagement and alumni relations
  - Financial services and business units in schools
  - School and teacher registration and accreditation.

A popular response to this complexity is to restructure leadership and management, employing more specialists in the different aspects of the school's operations. Ironically, this increases the complexity.

The following list is a handful of the new positions created at Hunter Valley Grammar School, from when I arrived in 2007 to my semi-retirement in 2020. The list is not exhaustive, but covers the new roles that readily come to mind:

- Compliance manager
- Human resources manager
- Director of ICT
- Director of rowing
- Farm manager (resident)
- Cafeteria manager
- Marketing manager
- Communications manager
- Alumni manager and archivist.

You will also need access to a lawyer who is familiar with the industry and sector.

I developed a partnership with the Sydney office of a law firm. I had an agreement under their legal workplace advisory service whereby I was able to submit an unlimited number of employment-law related queries via an online platform, telephone or email and receive support from their lawyers. At my request, I could also receive written advice of up to two pages in length for each query/matter; and they would review legal documents of up to a total of five pages in length for each query/matter.

I had a senior associate, Danika (also an alumnus of the school) at the end of a mobile when I needed her.

I am using this example as one way to respond to the complexities of leading, large, autonomous independent schools.

Many schools are entering into virtual services for information technology, human resources, financial services, marketing and public relations. I did this at my last school. Our budget was not substantial enough to employ a range of specialists in all areas, so it served the school well. This is another example of why principals are CEOs. They have to run their schools as businesses using the systems and approaches for services common in business.

It is worth mentioning that schools who are members of the state-based associations of independent schools get human resource and industrial relations advice as part of the membership. This is invaluable for you as a principal.

There are many services agreement options available to schools these days. These can include virtual services, bursarial (and financial services), communications and marketing, human resources, information technology and others. Under an annual service fee, the providers give you ongoing support to cover a skills gap, build capacity or smooth an uneven workload. These service agreement models mean you can retain one or two core staff at the administration/officer level and seek high-end supports from the virtual services. Servicing schools in the 2020s is big business, with very good providers in the market. Making good decisions about who to work with is imperative.

Changes in complexity

Independent schools are complex systems, irrespective of their size. However, the bigger a school, the more complex it becomes. The table below illustrates the complexity of the schools that were involved in my research. The principals of these schools manage large annual operational budgets ranging from $25M to over $70M. They are also responsible for large capital budgets – during the three-year period I gathered data, these ranged from $20M to $50M.

Circumstances	Centenary	Founders	Waterview	Regional
	Karleen	Allan	Karen	Adam
ICSEA[3]	1184	1132	1143	1064
Annual income (2017)	$70M	$66M	$38M	$28M
Capital (2015-2017)	$51M	$50M	$21M	$18M
Enrolments (2017)	2,203	2,026	1,500	1,411
Employees, FTE[4] (2017)	322	281	192	167
Complexity	Four sub-schools	Three campuses on three sites	Four sub-schools, two campuses on two sites	Four sub-schools and a working farm

I want to highlight the distinction between complexity and complicated. Schools are complex systems. Complex systems are far more difficult to manage than merely complicated ones. It's harder to predict what will happen in a complex system because they the elements within a complex system interact in unexpected ways. Schools are comprised of people, and how they interact, respond, and behave can be highly unpredictable.

When working with people, I saw behaviours I had never experienced and could not understand from my own world view. The behaviours I saw at times surprised me and there were times when I didn't know how to deal with them. I found it hard to anticipate outcomes, because what happened in the past may not predict a future behaviour. I found that an outlier, something you didn't see coming, is often far more significant and impactful then the norm.

It's easy to confuse the merely complicated with the genuinely complex. Managers need to know the difference. I like to advise colleagues that if they manage their school, a complex organisation, as if it were just a complicated one, they'll make serious, expensive mistakes.

One finding of my research was that principals in large, independent schools in Australia today face increasing complexity, change and diversity. Leading large, complex, multi-faceted, autonomous, independent schools in Australia requires significant leadership intelligence, knowledge and experience.

There are other aspects of these schools that further illustrate the complexity of the role for these principals. They must:

- Manage significant land holdings, assets, property, plant and equipment. Regional owns 38 hectares of land and Centenary has 20 hectares, Waterview has two campuses and Regional three campuses. These are substantial landholdings
- Sustain considerable financial foundations to ensure they have the resources for capital projects. These schools do not receive Australian government funding for capital projects
- Lead and manage multiple stakeholder groups, including affiliated churches, past students' associations, parents and friends' associations, and parent support groups for various co-curricular programs and activities
- Manage wide-reaching legal and compliance issues
- Have extensive school events and functions, clubs and activities, international service programs, and host international staff and student groups
- Sustain the school's unique brand and reputation to meet enrolment targets and guarantee the school remains viable
- Manage affiliated businesses, including performing arts centres available to the public; early learning centres, outside school hours care facilities; cafeterias and dining halls; and uniform shops.

A systems-thinking approach

To help manage the complexity of the schools where I was principal, I adopted a systems-thinking approach. I learned to understand my school as a set of complex interactions among its many interconnected parts. Everything needed to work together for the entire school and its operations to perform successfully. To begin to wrap your head around this, ask yourself: What is your business? Do you understand all of the parts and how they work seamlessly together?

It took some time, but as my experience developed, I could see how all the separate parts needed to come together. The conductor has to ensure that all sections of the orchestra play beautiful music when they come together. They work on their sectional scores independent of each other to know their part, and then the conductor draws them together.

Here are a few examples of the areas where synergies had to exist:

- Effective marketing and positive public relations lead to interest in the school, which impacts on enrolments
- Astute financial management ensures that assets and resources are available to support quality student programs and activities
- The grounds team mobilised all resources and prioritised the grounds, lawns and gardens weeks before an open day, to have the school spick and span
- School theatrical productions required significant commitment and enthusiasm from teaching staff, reception, marketing and communications and grounds, to name a few.

The most successful principals view their school as a system, thinking holistically about the component parts that make up the organisation. One case study principal also used the conductor metaphor:

> We are like a conductor; we are not playing the instruments. But it is the head's job to get the orchestra together and to play beautiful music together.

To be effective, I knew I had to successfully manage all aspects of the operation with the future firmly in my mind and the financial viability of the school steadfastly in my strategic thinking.

One case study principal described how effectiveness was measured by her acumen across all areas of operations: business, financial and project management, and education.

The key lesson here is that it is the principal's job to provide principled and decisive leadership across all areas of the school. Do not shy away from this or shirk the challenges. To ensure that you are effective as a principal, you must have the courage and resilience to provide robust and uncompromising leadership and effective supervision and management across a wide range of diverse areas.

After the annual golf day at one of my schools, two parents asked me when we would have agriculture at our school. Twelve months later, our school was the owner of a 20-acre mixed farm. The farm was acquired to teach agriculture, cattle team, and as a small business. I employed a farm manager with thirty years of industry experience. That was a steep learning curve for a principal whose father was a postmaster in rural towns where he was the only labour supporter. Despite living in rural areas, I had little or no context for the working farm and what was required, yet here I was, the CEO looking after a farm. From that December I was the godfather to cattle, goats and sheep, and I was meant to know about crops, fertiliser and pesticides. It became a flagship program and as a crucial aspect of the school's operations, I needed to know it.

Prive (2021) claims that this is where management stops, and leadership starts:

- Management controls the day-to-day operations
- Management focuses on deadlines
- Management solves immediate problems
- Leadership envisions a new future
- Leadership creates a pathway forward
- Leadership solves problems
- Leadership inspires change.

It's easy to assume that you need to choose to either be a leader or a manager. That's not the case; you have to do both. The best leaders in the world have known when to step out of the management role and into leadership.

I didn't see myself leading in one area, distinct to another. I knew I had to shoulder responsibility and accept accountability for the school's performance in all areas. I could identify a challenge in any area, and I knew to ask the right questions and seek solutions.

The table below illustrates what it looks like to lead and manage a whole school. It is much more than dealing with curriculum and assessment. It is a juggling act and requires knowing how to prioritise the competing demands for your time and energy.

Organisation-wide leading and managing in schools	
Leading	Managing
Self	Operations
Staff development	The whole organisation
Student outcomes	Complex relationships
Educatonal programs	The image and reputation of the school
Change and innovation	The school's future viability
Community	The spirtual dimension (in faith-based schools)

How do you learn to manage complexity?

Experience is a great teacher. As you gather your own experiences, your colleagues can offer sage advice. Seek out information from your independent schools' association and the peak body for independent school principals in Australia, AHISA. Best of all, talk to the people who run the various sections of your school, have high quality dialogue, listen and learn. Remember, you are the CEO; you don't need to know how to shear a sheep.

Experience is the sum of your leadership journey, your pathway, the ongoing professional learning, opportunities to sit on committees in your schools, including board sub-committees, a deliberate purposeful plan for development and growth. Which leadership positions do you apply for and accept, in which schools, learning from which principals?

Having your own professional coach who knows your aspirations and wants to walk beside you in helping you realise your goals is a critical step.

One effective strategy that I used to ensure successful whole-school operations was to work hard to ensure that the learning for each individual staff member was geared toward enabling them to enhance the school's overall effectiveness.

I took the lead to ensure that all staff knew the part they played in:

- Being an advocate for the school
- Maintaining a favourable public image of the school
- Providing quality communications with key stakeholders
- Delivering a good customer experience for parents and visitors
- Knowing how to work collegially as part of a team.

I did this through the dialogue I had with my staff, every day; the writing I did for the newsletter and other publications; public speeches at ceremonies and events; leading the whole of staff gatherings and meetings; and encouraging staff to be part of networks and broader learning communities.

While I was engaged in leading learning about teaching and learning, I also made sure that my staff knew what was involved in being part of a large, complex organisation.

At the start of each term, during the pupil free day(s) I would, without fail, introduce the new term with an address to all staff, making sure that there were at least five things staff would find interesting and motivating. I had to build a sense of whole staff, not the factions that can often occur between teaching and non-teaching staff, or staff from different departments.

Schools are becoming more complex, in part due to the ongoing changes with regulations, politics, business plans, technology investments and more. There are several government acts which overlay a significant degree of compliance adding to the complexity as well. The impact of these acts on schools in the current compliance climate is intense. Schools must demonstrate and show evidence of compliance.

As a principal in an independent school in NSW, the following are just some of the state and federal legislations that impacted my work:

- Child Protection (Working with Children) Act 2012
- Work, Health and Safety Act 2011
- Anti-Discrimination Act 1977
- Fair Work Act 2009
- Australian Education Act 2013
- Government Information (Public Access) Act 2009.

It is a principal's job to manage the growing complexity in schools and not overwhelm staff. You are a gatekeeper for staff.

As schools "expand" they inevitably become more complex. Their organisational structures develop layers upon layers, their reporting lines become tangled, and their people – from senior management through to the teacher in front of the class – find it harder to get work done. When time, energy, and resources are spent on activities and interactions that don't create value for children and teachers, complexity starts to damage a school's performance.

Five strategies for managing complexity

1. *Know what your employees actually do*
   This seems simple enough, but I have seen principals who don't know their staff, let alone what they do. You are supposed to know what people do and why they do it.

   When you don't engage or interact with your staff frequently, you miss lots of opportunities to optimise productivity and improve staff feelings about their work and your school.

   The better you can understand your employees, the easier it will be to keep them fulfilled and satisfied with their work.

2. *Support the "bus drivers"*
   The bus drivers are staff who have the interest, commitment and positivity to influence others on the bus.

   Find ways to empower staff who naturally encourage other staff and inspire them to commit and improve. The more empowered they are, the more they'll positively influence your school's culture.

   Affirm their work by public recognition of the good they're doing for the school as a whole. Make sure you're specific and detailed with your praise so others can model that same behaviour.

3. *Give more people more influence*
   The real key to performance is combining cooperation with autonomy. The mistake that principals can make with standard approaches to an increasingly complex environment is to create new layers, processes

and systems to deal with the challenges. When you do that, you can also sacrifice people's autonomy. That makes your school/organisation less agile.

Agility in leadership is one of the most powerful leadership models that I know. I tried to exercise agile leadership in my roles. This isn't the place to discuss agile leadership, but I do recommend De Smet, Lurie, and St George (2018):

> Agile organizations, viewed as living systems, have evolved to thrive in an unpredictable, rapidly changing environment. These organisations are both stable and dynamic. They focus on customers, fluidly adapt to environmental changes, and are open, inclusive, and non-hierarchical; they evolve continually and embrace uncertainty and ambiguity. Such organisations, we believe, are far better equipped than traditional ones for the future.

Other notable contributors to the field include Breakspear (2017), Kozak-Holland (2009), Owens and Valesky (2007) and Yukl (2010).

I wanted my people to feel that they could take risks, interpret rules and use their judgment and intelligence. I tried to give my leaders the authority to make decisions in my schools and the responsibility to carry them through. I wanted them to solve problems on their own, and then come to me and have a good chat about the problem and what their solution was. Or to chat to me at intervals in solving the problem so I could be a reference and a resource.

It was important in my leadership of direct reports and leaders in general, that they could choose when they work and how the work gets done. I found it could make a huge difference in how much effort they put into their work. I stayed close and held them accountable.

4. *Hold your staff accountable*
   My leaders worked a whole lot better when they understood and had to live with the consequences of their decision. They were sharper when they knew there was accountability.

People want to know how the work they do fits into the bigger picture; you have to lead them into this realisation. If people focus on performing the duties they've been tasked with, oblivious to how their work impacts the quality of the products or the people they work with, they tend to add little or no value to the organisation's achievements.

I knew that when I held leaders to account for the consequences of their decisions, they understood how their work fitted into the entire system. They would make fewer mistakes and paid more attention to their work quality.

5. *Accept mistakes for good tries*
    If people are afraid to fail, they'll hide issues from you and your peers. Reward people who bring problems to the surface – and address those who don't come together to help solve them.

    Leaders with low emotional intelligence can poison your culture with arrogant and overly dismissive behaviour. A toxic work environment fosters distrust and destroys morale. Less-confident employees become afraid to speak up for fear of being criticised and shunned. Others become cynical. This can result in everyone being too busy watching their own back to care about the company.

    If your employees don't alert you to issues, your organisation's problems will likely go unnoticed until they become critical and disrupt your day-to-day business operations. It is your job to ensure your workplace culture rewards people who expose issues.

    When an employee presents a problem, demonstrate your willingness to analyse and evaluate the situation in an unbiased, non-judgemental manner. Address problem employees by establishing boundaries and calling them out on their inappropriate behaviour in a logical and non-confrontational way.

    Present them with evidence to back up what you're saying and be firm about your expectations going forward, as well as what the consequences are should they refuse to act professionally.

    Accept mistakes if staff are genuinely trying new ideas and trying to be innovative.

In hindsight

All schools must grow, not necessarily in size but in new programs, products and services for children, development of teachers, and authentic involvement of parents. You want to grow your school's cognitive capacity – how your staff, as a whole, use cognitive skills to solve problems, and to think, learn and improve the quality of programs and services.

THE SCHOOL'S FUTURE IS IN YOUR HANDS

Principals in independent schools in Australia are responsible for establishing their school's point of difference and sustaining this in the market-driven context. As a principal you are building an image of a child's future.

The management of brand/image is an integral part of your role as the principal, but it adds to the pressure of the position. If you don't manage the brand of your school, then your school can be unviable. You have a responsibility to see that all staff in your school support this aspect of the school and engage with the associated obligation to ensure that the school is held in high esteem in the community.

Don't let your staff tell you they aren't partly responsible for the PR and marketing of the school – that somehow this belongs with the marketing team. Everyone on the staff of an independent school is responsible for the reputation of the school. What they say and do, how they behave, interact and represent themselves, it all reflects the school they work in. Every single interaction counts.

I expected my staff to make sure that every interaction was positive, favourable and enduring. I set the example – each time I found myself interacting with a parent, prospective parent, potential employee, donor or other person of influence, I made sure I was:

- Genuine
- Able to leave an impression
- True to my values and beliefs
- Intentional
- Considerate
- Curious.

Despite my best efforts, there were inevitably times that interactions that didn't go so well.

It isn't uncommon for a principal to have to deal with parents who had their fees fall into arrears. The bursar's team would usually deal with this, until the parent refused to respond or cooperate with the bursar, then it would get escalated.

I recall a parent who had allowed their debt to fall into arrears by more than six months. At the start of the new school year, the matter had already been handed over to a debt collection agency because the parent refused to speak to our finance team. I asked the parent to meet with me to discuss the situation.

Without notice to me, the parent brought with them a newly elected director. It became obvious after about 5 minutes that he wanted to impress the parent and show he was a good representative on the board.

The parent made the case for why I should apply grace in her situation, pleading that the child's learning and development would suffer if I didn't sustain the enrolment and allow the debt to be paid over the full year.

I was my usual friendly self, listening, understanding, waiting for the time to make my point – that I need to have outstanding fees paid by entering into a reliable fee payment plan.

The parent began setting the conditions of payment of the debt and instructing me on how I would respond, but the discussion really turned when the parent announced, "I will work constructively and collaboratively with the school and [board member] and the board on this matter."

The board member jumped in, asserting his role and what he would be doing as the policeman to monitor my response and action.

I called a halt to my mild-mannered behaviour at that point. I had candid words for the director and the parent. I said to the board member, "[name], you have no role here today, other than to be a support person and you have no role after this meeting."

And to the parent, "[name], you will work with me; this is not a board matter, and I will determine whether your arrangements are acceptable to the school and what action I will take, including terminating the enrolment of [child]."

The meeting ended soon after that.

What is the lesson from this? There are times when, despite the best-intentioned plans, copybook manner and conduct, you are required to call a spade a spade. The key is knowing when to call things out.

Strategic leadership

Strategic leadership is a must for effective leaders.

You can improve your strategic leadership by working on your strategic thinking skills. Strategic thinking is not just for the principal or board. It is part of any executive leader's role.

When I was developing my strategic leadership, I would seek out and observe developments in other schools, systems and countries. You must lift your head from your desk and watch external trends and initiatives. To be strategic, you need a solid understanding of the independent school's context, trends and success drivers.

I made it a routine exercise to pay attention to the issues that would get raised repeatedly in my school and analysed the common obstacles to innovation that my staff seemed to be facing.

As I have already discussed, I was proactive about connecting with peers in my network, nationally and internationally, to understand what was happening that could make a difference in my school.

I would ask tough questions of my executive leaders and board. I was curious, always looking at information from different points of view. This enabled me to see other possibilities, approaches and potential outcomes.

As a strategic thinker, I would challenge the status quo and get people talking about underlying assumptions. Those that are really skilled at strategic thinking can walk people through the process of identifying issues, shaping common understanding, and framing strategic choices.

Making time for thinking and strategising is essential. You must give quality time in your executive meetings to thinking about your school's future. Encourage debate and invite your team to challenge what you do, why you do it the way you do, and what things could look like if done differently.

Focus on issues, not people, and use neutral peers to challenge your thinking.

Strategic leadership is a mindset and can be developed through conscious action and practice.

The best leaders do not spend too much time in short-term strategic plans. The three-to-five-year planning, which is all too common in most organisations, is not long-sighted enough. The best leaders are always thinking strategically, planning the future of their organisations ten-to-fifteen years into the future.

Aspiring principals ask me how I decide what is good for a school in ten-to-fifteen years' time. And how do I work towards it, knowing that I will more than likely be gone by then.

When I think fifteen years ahead, I am thinking of the school in terms of systems-level evolution. I am thinking about what disruptions could happen to unsettle how we, as a school, are operating. What could force us to rethink our way of doing things, the educational programs we offer, the staffing expertise we might require. I do a lot of work researching how schools and the education industry must evolve to meet the challenges of new technology, market forces, regulation and the like. I know if I am not thinking about that, then someone else will be in a position to dictate the terms of my future. And I don't want that. My thinking is about the direction in which I hope the school and the education industry will evolve.

The best leaders are not waiting for their boards to initiate a strategic planning process, they have a clear futures perspective, plotting the future. Effective principals bring their boards into the thinking and planning at the right time and bring them in judiciously so that from the first, the engagement is authentic and validates the school's values, beliefs, mission and purpose.

There is no doubt in my mind that it is your job to plan your school's future. Your school's destiny is in your hands. Your leadership can have positive, enduring benefits and can leave a healthy legacy. However, if you are ineffectual, you will put your school's viability at risk.

Any organisation's sustainability and long-term viability requires making wise and forward-thinking decisions now; and this is the role of the CEO.

The strategic priorities set by the CEO are developed from their compelling purpose for the organisation. It is your job to know what your organisation will look like in fifteen years.

At one of my schools, in the bayside suburbs of a capital city, we had ten good quality independent schools within a 10km radius. Sustaining market share was hard work, it really was. Especially when we were considered a "high-fee" school against the competitors. We were an all-girls' schools, with many of our competitors being co-educational. Our families who had boys sent them to two very large, independent boys' schools in the catchment. The mind-set of parents in the late 1990s and early 2000s was shifting toward co-educational schooling, as the most natural learning environment for all children. I knew I had to change our offerings to ensure our school's sustainability, so I did. I built a boys' school from scratch, just 2km away. And so, without merging two schools and creating a co-educational school, I provided two schools that were accessible to each other, offering many of the tangible benefits of a co-education. I felt this was an important strategic decision.

You are a visionary, or need to be

Leaders have asked me what a visionary leader looks like, how they think, what they do.

This is a fair question, and there is no simple response or blueprint that you can overlay on a leader's thinking.

At the most fundamental level, you've got to have a clear, visible picture of the future of your school. Then, you have to be able to lay out concrete steps to bring your vision to life. You'll need all the traits of good leadership to lead your community and your executive team in the direction you want to take the school.

I had a colleague at a school that found their market share was being whittled away, year after year. They were a high fee-paying school relative to the competitors in the town of around 6000 people. I encouraged my colleague to convince his board to implement a five-year plan to close the gap between the fees his school was charging and those being charged by his competitors. This meant that he had to develop annual business plans that had fee increases each year of less than half the increases of his competitor schools. At the same time, my colleague and I discussed the concept of value proposition. We interrogated the value of what he was promising to deliver to parents. I was able to help my colleague connect "value" to his school's overall marketing strategy. Together we came up with key messages and declarations of intent, statements that introduced prospective parents to what his school stood for, how it operated, and why it deserved the enrolment of their child. He had to convince interested parents why they should "buy" his school over competitors.

It was an intense process, but we got there – the school now has waiting lists and runs a surplus. This was visionary on the part of my colleague.

You can't begin to act like a visionary leader unless you can break from what's expected. I always tried to lead with intention and enthusiasm in a way that made my staff, board and parents happy to follow.

I just wouldn't settle for "good enough." I wanted to try new things, find new opportunities, and know how to stay the course. I knew I had to be resilient and resolute. I never gave up, even when things got difficult. I never stopped trying, never stopped floating ideas like kites. I was happy to listen to my people and jump on any good idea. I didn't have all the ideas, but there were plenty of people telling me what I needed to do. My job was to separate the wheat from the chaff. Effective principals can turn vision into ideas, and ideas into action.

Colleagues would say I was tough and determined and I was not easily intimidated. I was prepared to fight policies and institutions that have been in place for a long time. I bucked the system and took on the bureaucrats. I was a shield for my staff, resisting pressures both internal and external. And I wasn't afraid of failure, either. My only fear was not trying. I tried to cultivate the same tenacity in my executive.

There are many good practices that visionary leaders exhibit. A couple of examples include:

- They begin a project with a clearly contemplated plan that includes everything from processes to staff analysis
- They are always looking for improvement. They actively seek out opportunities to create buy-in from employees by improving organisational structures

- They share the vision with the right people at the right time. They invite others to give input and ideas, so the vision is shared and not just the property of one person.

Sustainability

Independent schools in Australia require parents to pay school fees; in many schools as much as 80 per cent of the required operating income can come from fees. The income covers the education of students and pays for the costs of managing medium/large, not-for-profit businesses.

If you fail to lead effectively, which means to sustain viable enrolment levels at your school, then your school's viability is threatened, which can result in school closure. Like the CEO of any corporation, the independent school principal must see that their school, as a business, is solvent and that its financial future is secure. This means meeting parents needs and expectations.

At one school where I was principal, the enrolments were flagging. With the admissions and marketing team working really hard to maintain our optimal roll, I knew we needed to provide something exceptional to children and families. My vision was to see the school as an International Baccalaureate (IB) World School in four programs: the primary years; the middle years; the diploma; and career-related programs. Why? Because I wanted our school to provide an educational program for our children and young adults that did so much more than the pedestrian and stifling state-based curricula. I wanted our students to experience an education that developed them as inquiring, knowledgeable and caring young people, an education that built students' critical thinking skills, that nurtured their curiosity and their ability to solve complex problems. I wanted the graduates of my school to be able to play their part in building a better world through intercultural understanding and respect, alongside a healthy appetite for learning and excellence. The IB programs do that. This was not meant to be a shameless promotion of the IB – the point is that you have to know what you want for your school for the long haul, and why.

The best principals are deeply invested in their school's future and viability; they make a long-term commitment to the school. Most principals I know want to stay in their new school for a long time; they know it takes three-to-five years to have a real impact and seven years to make sustained change. They want to leave a legacy that will see the school successful beyond their own time. This requires you as the principal to be focused on the future, hold a quantifiable vision for the school's future, engage your community in realising the vision, and continuously strive to see that the school performs at its best.

I always accepted that the school's destiny, and future, was where I could take it as principal. I had significant authority vested in me by my boards. I knew my leadership could have positive and enduring benefits and leave a healthy legacy. I also knew that if I didn't cut it, I could put the school's viability at risk.

Enrolments are a fair KPI

Whether sustainable enrolments are set as a formal KPI or not, it is a core performance measure that you would do well to assign to yourself.

Thinking like a CEO, I knew how critical it was to maintain a sustainable enrolment base to ensure the future viability of the school. I knew it was my responsibility to ensure market-share was sustained, resulting in the school's long-term viability and success.

Before you begin this evaluation and consider appropriate action, you must know your competitors. I did a competitor analysis, enlisted the services of a local demographer, threw satisfaction surveys at parents, held parent forums, asked business and community leaders what expectations they held of an "elite" private school in the city – I did everything I could to understand the school's context, community expectations and what the school needed most.

At the same time, I made sure that our educational programs, campus environment, reputation and teaching staff were so good that my school was highly sought after by parents seeking enrolment. This takes investment, both fiscal and people.

I wanted my school to be considered the best option for parents in the catchment market. I looked beyond the next five-to-ten years; my eyes were on the long-term success of my schools for generations to come.

Factors for long-term success

- My leadership and professional reputation had the greatest impact on enrolments
- Ensuring that every child, parent, staff and visitor had a quality experience
- Parents and community had to know that I had a vision for the school grounded in a school-improvement paradigm
- Build a top-quality faculty and staff, the envy of other schools in the area
- Unrivalled customer service to ensure high levels of parent satisfaction
- Our reputation had to create high-energy conversations in the wider community
- I knew our demography, our context, our value proposition, and I knew what our families wanted
- Our competitors were watching us, I didn't watch them
- I reached out to service providers to deepen and strengthen the expertise I had in my school.

Restless

The best principals I know are restless (Blatchford, 2014) – they want to get better; they wanted to keep improving. They do not accept the status quo; they create a sense of urgency about what needs to be done. They challenge entrenched practices and behaviours and respond to local and global challenges. Blatchford (2014) claimed that "successful schools are restless schools." They are restless to get better.

I was always seeking out changes in the education landscape that could have a bearing on my school, and I would bring that knowledge into my own improvement agenda. Being effective as a principal meant I had to provoke change and navigate the school's future as a means to manage the complex, competitive and volatile educational world.

Whenever I went into a new school (after the appropriate settling in period) I would interrogate the way things were done – routines, practices, systems and protocols. I have never had difficulty confronting comfortable customs and practices that existed in my schools. Where necessary, I purposefully challenged what was going on, from routines to culture.

The most successful principals I know lead, motivate and manage change, and lead for continuous improvement. They do that by being agile, flexible and adapting to the school's changing context. They don't sit still.

This is achieved by using a combination of research, reading, ideas obtained from colleagues and their learned associations, and trusting your instincts and intuitions accumulated from years of experience. I often knew instinctively what needed attention and what needed to be done. I had an insatiable appetite for change and transformation, for seeking to make our school the best that it could be.

Martin Luther King, in Phillips (2001), sums it up for me in stating that leaders:

1. Do not sugar-coat reality
2. Engage the heart
3. Refuse to accept the status quo
4. Create a sense of urgency
5. Call people to act in accord with their highest values
6. Refuse to settle
7. Acknowledge the sacrifice of their followers
8. Paint a vivid picture of a better tomorrow.

I felt that one of the most vital strategies that I could use to sustain my school's future viability was to ensure that the school was projected in an extremely positive light in the broader community, and that prospective parents found the school appealing and wanted their child enrolled.

My experience has taught me that it is a whole lot easier to plan your school's future, think strategically and implement your plans and aspirations if you stay the course for the long haul. "A rolling stone gathers no moss." If you don't stay put in your school for more than five years, it is hard to see your vision for the school come to fruition.

A bright-eyed, twelve-year-old girl made me sit up in an interview and think about longevity, from various angles. I was interviewing year 6 students for a place in year 7, and would always ask the children if they had any questions for me. This girl, who would have to travel to school 40 minutes by bus every day asked me, "Mr. Teys, will you still be my principal when I graduate in year 12?"

Wow! That was confronting. I was about seven years into my term as principal and knew that I may very well not be. I thought long and hard about my reply, and then it came out: "I would love to be." She said, "I would love that too."

And I was there. It was an emotional moment at her graduation when she reminded me of the "promise" I had made and kept. Her graduation prompted me to reflect on what we had achieved together, and I knew that it wouldn't have been possible if I hadn't been there for a long innings.

In hindsight

I knew it was my job to plot the school's future. I was responsible for planning and executing critical strategic decisions to ensure the school's future was buoyant. I felt my role was to act as custodian of the school's heritage and torch bearer for its future. This might sound vain, but it isn't meant to be – it is the role. Your whole community will expect this of you.

After more than twenty years as a principal, I have concluded that leading and managing the school's brand and image with confidence and adeptness is a crucial aspect of the role. The principal's effectiveness in this impacts on the school's financial viability. It is crucial that all I do as the principal and leader must enhance the image and reputation of the school.

I wanted and needed my schools to have an excellent reputation that spoke to the quality of my school in the broader community and to the hearts and minds of prospective parents. If I seemed preoccupied with this component of my leadership, it is because I appreciated the gravity of the cost if I neglected it.

Chapter notes

3. ICSEA – Index of Community Socio-Educational Advantage. ICSEA provides an indication of the socio-educational backgrounds of students. The national average is 1000.
4. FTE – full-time equivalent

CONCLUSION

My aim in writing this book was to provide a resource that could contribute in a significant way to the knowledge and understanding of contemporary leadership provided by the principal in large, P–12, autonomous, independent schools in Australia.

Colleagues, and aspirants, have asked me how a principal learns to be a principal in these schools. I sought professional learning opportunities that were relevant to my leadership context, and I was judicious in choosing experiences that would impact my leadership. I believe this book has helped in answering this question.

I hope that by reading this book, you have found clarity around what is required to be an effective principal in large, P–12, autonomous, independent schools in Australia. I trust that you have appreciated the perspectives and insights that I have shared from my own experiences and my thesis. In my view, effective principal leadership is vital for the survival and viability of the independent school sector in Australia. If we are not able to provide quality succession planning for a generation of principals who will leave the sector, then we put at risk the viability and allure of independent schools. It became apparent to me in completing my research that the principal in an independent school in Australia has a profound impact on the performance of the school as a company, an educational organisation, a business, and as a producer of quality graduates. Principals in autonomous independent schools are the agent for the school's success, and boards have a critical responsibility to choose the right person for the job and ensure the success of that appointment through ongoing support, nurture and development.

The completion of my research changed me and my view of principalship in independent schools. It heightened my determination to ensure that quality professional development, collegial supports and coaching of principals is readily available to support the vital work they perform for their school communities.

REFERENCES

Association of Heads of Independent Schools Australia (2011) AHISA's Model of autonomous school principalship. https://www.ahisa.edu.au/AHISA/Resources/Professional_resources/Principalship_Model/AHISA/Resources/Professional_resources/Principalship_Model.aspx?hkey=05efeaa1-1790-4d54-b475-1f10fd2046e4

Blackwood B (14 June 2019) 'What it takes to lead', *Australian Financial Review*. https://www.afr.com/policy/health-and-education/what-it-takes-to-lead-20190612-p51wwz

Blatchford R (2014) *The restless school* John Catt Educational Ltd (UK).

Branson R (2015) *The Virgin way* Ebury Publishing (UK).

Breakspear S (2017) 'Embracing agile leadership for learning: How leaders can create impact despite growing complexity', *Australian Educational Leader* 39(3): 68–71.

Brown B (2018) *Dare to lead* Vermilion (UK).

Bunn M (2010) *Ancient wisdom for modern health: Rediscover the simple, timeless secrets of health and happiness* Enlightened Health Publishing (Australia).

Burdo A (2017) Michelle Obama tells 12,000 in Philly: "Speak up", *Philadelphia Business Journal* https://www.bizjournals.com/washington/bizwomen/news/latest-news/2017/10/michelle-obama-tells-12-000-in-philly-speak-up.html

Collins J (2001) *Good to great* HarperBusiness (UK),

Day C, & Gurr D (Eds) (2014) L*eading schools successfully: Stories from the field* Routledge (UK).

Davies B (2014) *Listening to children: Being and becoming* Routledge (UK).

Degenhardt L (2015) 'Leadership directions: Finding a leadership compass for a complex world', *Independence*, 40(2): 6–8.

De Smet A, Lurie M, & St George A (2018) *Leading agile transformation: The new capabilities leaders need to build 21st-century organizations* McKinsey & Company.

Scroggs L (n.d.) Time blocking (accessed 2021) https://todoist.com/productivity-methods/time-blocking

Drucker (1988) The coming of the new organization, *Harvard Business Review*, 66, 45–53.

Drysdale L, Bennett J, Murakami E, Johansson O & Gurr D (2014), Heroic leadership in Australia, Sweden, and the United States, *International Journal of Educational Management*, 28(7) 785–797.

Duckworth AL, Peterson C, Matthews MD, & Kelly DR (2007) 'Grit: Perseverance and passion for long-term goals', *Journal of personality and social psychology*, 92(6): 1087.

Duckworth A L (2022) https://angeladuckworth.com/

Evers JLH (2013) 'It's not the critic who counts, but the man in the arena', *Human Reproduction*, 28(2): 287.

Fiorina, C (2021) https://www.linkedin.com/pulse/people-watch-walk-carly-fiorina/

Fraser A (2012) *The third space* Random House (Australia).

Fullan M (2011) *Change leader: Learning to do what matters most* John Wiley & Sons (USA).

Goe L (2007) 'The link between teacher quality and student outcomes: A research synthesis', *National Comprehensive Centre for Teacher Quality*, October 2007.

Governance Institute of Australia (2015) *Adding value to school governance: Toolkit*, 15–18.

Greenleaf RK (1970) *The servant as leader* Robert Greenleaf Centre (USA).

Kelly G (2017) *Live, lead, learn* Penguin (Australia).

Munroe, K (18 Aug 2022) "Bespoke education": Are Australia's private schools worth the price tag? *The Guardian*. https://www.theguardian.com/australia-news/2018/aug/18/bespoke-education-are-australias-private-schools-worth-the-price-tag

Hargreaves A & Fink D (2006) *Sustainable leadership* John Wiley & Sons (USA).

Heijer D (2019) https://julieparkerpracticesuccess.com/when-a-flower-doesnt-bloom-you-fix-the-environment-in-which-it-grows-not-the-flower/

Independent Schools Australia (2021) https://isa.edu.au/about-independent-schools/school-statistics/

ISCA (2020) *Independent schooling in Australia snapshot 2019* https://isa.edu.au/snapshot-2020/

Kozak-Holland M (2009) *Agile leadership and the management of change: Project lessons from Winston Churchill and the Battle of Britain* Multi-Media Publications (Canada).

Murray G (2021) 'Why do we wake around 3am and dwell on our fears and shortcomings?' *The Conversation* https://theconversation.com/why-do-we-wake-around-3am-and-dwell-on-our-fears-and-shortcomings-169635

North B, Gross M, & Smith S (11 Sept 2015) 'Study confirms HSC exams source of major stress to adolescents', *The Conversation* https://theconversation.com/study-confirms-hsc-exams-source-of-major-stress-to-adolescents-46812#:~:text=When%20pressure%20was%20high%2C%2041,of%20both%20for%20gifted%20students.

Owens RG & Valesky TC (2007) *Organisational behaviour in education: Adaptive leadership and school reform* Pearson Education (USA).

Phillips DT (2001) *Martin Luther King, Jr., on leadership: Inspiration and wisdom for challenging times* Grand Central Publishing (USA).

Prive T (2021) https://www.inc.com/tanya-prive/where-does-management-stops-leadership-start.html

McEwan EK (2003) *10 traits of highly effective principals: From good to great performance* Corwin Press (USA).

Mulford D (2018) 'Measuring success of an independent school', *Independence* 43(1): 68-69.

Queenwood School for Girls (2013) Principal candidate information. In *Queenwood School for Girls* (Ed.) Cordiner King (Australia).

Riley P, See SM, Marsh H, & Dicke T (2021) *The Australian principal occupational health, safety and wellbeing Survey 2020 Data* Health & Wellbeing. https://www.healthandwellbeing.org/reports/AU/2020_AU_Final_Report_Embargoed.pdf

Schein EH (2004) *Organizational culture and leadership* (3rd ed.) Jossey-Bass (USA).

Sharma R (2018) *The 5 AM club: Own your morning, elevate your life* Harper Collins Publishers (Canada).

Stronge JH, Richard HB, & Catano N (2008) *Qualities of effective principals* ASCD (USA).

Simpson J (2021) https://www.afr.com/work-and-careers/education/big-schools-are-big-businesses-and-need-to-be-run-accordingly-20211121

Sutcliffe J (2013) *8 qualities of successful school leaders: The desert island challenge* Bloomsbury Publishing (UK).

Teys PF (2021) *Leading large, P-12, autonomous, independent schools: An Australian case study* [Unpublished, A thesis submitted for the award of Doctor of Education]. University of Southern Queensland.

Townsville Grammar School (2017) Appointment of principal. In *Townsville Grammar School* (Ed.) Odgers Berndtson (Australia).

Trice HM, & Beyer JM (1991) 'Cultural leadership in organizations', *Organization science*, 2(2): 149–169.

Watson L (2005) *Quality teaching and school leadership: A scan of research findings* Teaching Australia, Australian Institute for Teaching and School Leadership (Australia).

Wolny N (2021) https://www.nickwolny.com/

Yukl GA (2010) *Leadership in organizations* (7th ed.) Pearson (USA).

www.ingramcontent.com/pod-product-compliance
Lightning Source LLC
Chambersburg PA
CBHW071204210326
41597CB00016B/1667